Confessions of a Baby Boomer

Memories
of things I haven't
forgotten yet

by Myron J. Kukla

Published in the United States by Lockport Enterprises Ltd. Holland, Mich.

All of the articles that appear in this work were originally published in *The Lakeshore Press.*

Library of Congress Cataloging-in Publication Data
Myron Kukla
Confessions of a Baby Boomer: Memories of things I haven't forgotten yet / by Myron J. Kukla

ISBN: 0-9665606-0-4

Lockport Enterprises Ltd.
Printed in the United States of America on acid-free paper.

Dedication

To my wife, Madeline, and sons Jason, Nathan and Matthew who really don't look like the illustrated family on the cover of this book, which they've pointed out to me several times. Here is a real picture of all of us. This group has provided me with countless hours of joy, love and fun over the years and to these people I dedicate this book.

The Kuklas: (l - r) Matthew, Madeline, Jason, Myron and Nathan.

Thanks and appreciation

First I'd like to thank my Mom and Dad, Mary and Stanley Kukla, who let me spend countless hours in my youth reading and dreaming instead of cutting grass and doing homework, which is the perfect training for a writer.

Others I need to thank are Julie Hoogland, Editor of the Lakeshore Press, for finding my columns funny enough to publish every week. I also want to thank Amy Strassburger, my assistant editor on the book, who not only put the commas in the right places, but also convinced me to publish the book in English instead of third century Mandarin, which had been my original plan.

A special thanks is in order for Chuck Ayers who took time out of his busy schedule as co-creator of the nationally syndicated comic strip "Crankshaft" and pencil artist for "Funky Winkerbean" to give this book some very funny pictures to look at if you can't read.

And finally, my thanks and appreciation to my readers and fans who have encouraged me with their letters and personal acknowledgments. It's for you I write these.

—Myron J. Kukla

Introduction

I don't know about you, but I'm getting a little tired of this "Baby Boomer" label I've had hung on me.

Just because we all happen to be born within a decade or so of 40 million other post-war kids, and we all share the same television and music memories that we now have in common with our 2.5 children thanks to cable TV and oldies stations, and just because we're all turning gray, flabby and bald at the same time, and most of us wish it was still the glory days between 1960 and 1976 when disco hit, but we were too busy to enjoy because we were all raising families and/or establishing careers that turned out to be dead ends, but which we missed once we got downsized, and had to re-enter the job market and color our hair, grow it long and curly, then cut it short like George Clooney and waif models, and start wearing bifocal contact lenses and weird shaped sunglasses, and spend thousands of dollars on exercise and aerobics tapes, and equipment so we could look like we were still in the game even though we never quite adjusted to the Information Age and often pay our kids to set the digital clock on the VCR, but we're happy because we've cracked the receiving part of e-mail and can now retrieve thousands of messages a day from people who think passing on Internet jokes is some form of communication, when, in reality, all we ever longed for was a windowed-office and a secretary with an IBM Selectric typewriter, but wound up with a cubicle, computer and voice mail and the woman who might have been our secretary is now the boss thanks to women's lib which men initially supported because, to them, it simply meant "braless women," but for females meant a career and emancipation from household drudgery, only the careers turned out to be just more work on top of home and family and not as much fun as it looked when they dreamed of becoming president of General Motors, but now is a necessity to support a home and try to build a nest egg for retirement because all those older people before us, who most of us call Mom and Dad, are using up the Social Security before we get there, and we're going to need something to fund our golden years at the trailer park just outside Orlando and be able to buy a few tablets of Viagra now and then.

Other than that, I don't think we have a whole lot in common. Besides, if we do I've probably forgotten it by now and so have you. That's why I wrote this stuff down.

Contents

Chapter VII

Chapter VIII

Chapter I

MY SHORT TERM MEMORY IS LONG GONE

This week, I lost my short term memory, talked to the dog, cleared my desk, saved $1.39 for retirement and discovered that life is like a broken VCR. Other than that, it was a pretty quiet week.

I believe part of my memory problem stems from the fact that there is just too much stuff in my head to remember. Too bad you can't download parts of your brain to a computer disk to clear out the files, or at least, suck out unused information with a vacuum cleaner.

MY SHORT TERM MEMORY IS LONG GONE

My wife and kids believe I have no short-term memory.

What was I saying?

Oh yeah, for some reason, my family thinks I've lost my short term ... what do you call it ... motor bike. Just kidding. I knew the word was memory, because I wrote it down the second time I forgot it.

I seem to have developed this memory problem shortly after I got married. I don't think getting married had anything to do with it. Or did it? I forget.

Anyway, I think part of the problem is there are many more people in my life to notice my memory lapses than when I was single. When I was single and I forgot something, it didn't matter because I couldn't remember that I forgot it. Life was simple, even exciting at times. People would show up on my doorstep dressed like zebras and I would have no memory of why they where there. "Who are you?" I'd ask. "And what are you doing on my doorstep dressed like zebras?" Unfortunately, I've forgotten what their answer was.

Life, though, got more complicated as my immediate family grew. Not only did I have to remember everything in my life, but also everything in their lives, too.

What day is it?

Face it, it's difficult to try to remember what you've got to do for yourself, let alone someone else. When we were first married, my wife, Madeline, would call me up every Thursday and say "you forgot to pick me up from work again!"

Embarrassed, I'd say, "I'm sorry honey, when was I supposed to pick you up?" And every time she'd reply "Tuesday" like I'm supposed to keep track of what day it is or something.

I've often suspected my family has taken advantage of my poor memory over the years. I know the kids used to try to get double and triple allowances off me by going "Dad, you forgot my allowance this week." Sometimes they'd get their allowance, change clothes and come back for more. I put a stop to it when they started bringing in neighborhood friends to get allowances, passing them off as children I'd forgotten.

And my wife Marilyn - I think that's her name - sometimes would show up with new clothes and jewelry I supposedly had bought her. "You said you bought it for the tenth anniversary of our second date," she would say. "Don't you remember?"

The funny thing is, I would probably remember doing something like that.

I believe part of my memory problem stems from the fact that there is just too much stuff in my head to remember. And most of it goes back to grade school. I've got the multiplication tables stored in there, proper long division, the Gettysburg Address (701 Leeside Drive, Gettysburg), lyrics to old Beatles songs, nursery rhymes, the correct spelling of thousands of words I never use like "perfunctory."

I've also got the home phone numbers of hundreds of family and friends stored in there. I call them often and go "Who are you and what's your phone number doing in my brain?" Long pause... "Oh, hi Mom."

So it's no wonder I can't remember anything new.

My wife, Madeline, if in fact that is her name, got so worried about my thinning memory that she encouraged me to get help one night at supper right in front of the kids.

"I'm afraid one of these days you're going to look up from dinner and not know who your children are," she said.

I said that was nonsense, wondering what this woman and her three kids were doing sitting at my dining room table.

So I went out and bought a memory book — "10 Days to a Better Memory." But I forgot where I put the book the first day.

"How can you lose a book on memory?" asked my wife — we'll call her Ashley.

"What book?" I replied. "And by the way, who are you?"

Cleaning house

I think what I need to do is a general house cleaning up there. Too bad you can't download parts of your brain to a computer disk to clear out the files, or at least, suck out unused information with a vacuum cleaner.

Over the years, though, I've learned some tricks and home remedies to help me remember things.

For example, many of us after a certain age have a difficult time remembering people's names. I've found that it's easy to remember names if you hang out at conventions and seminars where everyone wears name tags. This is also helpful at home, as my wife Meredith can attest.

On one occasion, a friend recommended I try a natural drug called Ginkoba, which is supposed to improve the memory. But I didn't bother getting it. The way I looked at it, I would probably forget to take the stuff, then buy more because I couldn't remember if it worked.

One thing I've learned to do that's helped improve my memory tremendously is writing notes to myself and creating lists of things I should do. For those of you with similar memory problems who want to use this technique, I've to got warn you about one pitfall. You have to date your notes.

I came across one the other day reminding me to buy my son a new car seat. Well, I bought the seat but, like kids do at a certain age, he felt he was too big to sit in a car seat. "Besides, Dad, I'm driving now," he explained.

"Well then," I said, "I'd better take back the tricycle I got you for Christmas. I don't suppose you want that either."

Despite having this motor bike problem, I've always been able to remember important family events like birthdays, anniversaries and Father's Day.

Except recently I've found even that part of my mind is heading out on vacation. To make sure I remember these occasions, I now use memory aides to help me. Like when my wife — let's say her name's Martha — had a birthday coming up recently, I tied a string around my finger so I wouldn't forget. When she asked me what the string was for, I told a white lie and said it was a reminder for me to buy more string, not wanting her to know the real reason.

I'm proud to say, the string system worked. I didn't forget her birthday this year, although she is still trying to figure out why I got her a ball of twine as a gift.

*The worst thing about working out of your house
is you never get any snow days off and it's
always your turn to make the coffee.*

HOME ALONE: THE NAKED TRUTH

I'm a telecommuter. That means I don't have to get up and drive anywhere to work in the morning. I just roll out of bed and I'm at work.

My home is my office, and my computer, fax machine, telephone and e- mail address connect me with the rest of the world.

Actually, working out of your home is just like any regular job, except there's no rush-hour traffic. And you can have a coffee break anytime you want one because there's no one there to say "Hey! Isn't that your third coffee break? When are you going to get some work done?"

Other than that it's just like a regular job. Except, if you get tired of working, you can lay down for a nap. Or maybe pop a movie in the VCR. Not that I do any of these things.

Well, maybe once in a while. Like I might rest my eyes, or catch a little of General Hospital if it's a slow day. Or take the dog for a walk if it's a nice day. Sometimes I wash the car. Read a book. Do yoga. But that's just so I can stay mentally sharp for work. Other than that, it's just like a regular job.

If you know anyone that works at home, then you know it's no bed of roses. For example, you never get any "snow days" off from work. And it's always your turn to make the coffee. Worst of all, there's no one to complain to. "Hey, why is it always my turn to make the coffee?" I shout to the deserted house.

No one to talk to

I think the worst part of working alone is not being able to interact with coworkers on the job. The best I can do is try to discuss current events with the dog.

ME: "How's it going, girl? Think you'll catch any squirrels today? Did you see the Piston's game last night? Wasn't that something?"

DOG: "Woof, woof."

I admit my collie may not be much of a conversationalist, but she's a great listener.

Besides the dog, I see the gas meter reader about once a month.

And then there's the UPS driver. We do coffee on occasion. And just last week I had a nice chat with this guy from Detroit who stopped at my house to get directions. I wouldn't let him go until he tried some of my fresh-baked cinnamon rolls.

Another bad thing about working at home is you're on the job 24 hours a day. People can call you up any hour of the day and ask for things you forgot to do and you've got no excuses. Sometimes I try anyway. "No, sorry, I think I left all that at the office. By gosh you're right, this is my office, I forgot."

Dressing to telecommute

When I first started working at home, I dressed just as if I were going to the office. I'd get up and put on a white shirt and tie, dress slacks and a sports coat. Then I'd walk across my living room to my office, take off the coat, loosen my tie and get to work. I did this because someone, somewhere, once told me that people can tell how you were dressed when they talked to you on the telephone. "They'll know if you're professionally dressed, just by the sound of your voice," they said.

Well, after about a week of working in business clothes without a single compliment on my attire, I gave up on the coat and started wearing casual shirts, but still with a tie. That lasted another week before the tie went, followed by the dress slacks and good shoes. Eventually, I got down to sweatshirts, jeans and ratty tennis shoes.

And you know what? Nobody noticed. Not a single person said: "Hey, get a tie on or I'm not talking to you."

I've become convinced I could talk to people on the telephone naked with a lamp shade on my head and no one would be the wiser. Unless, of course, I give it away by giggling when I'm on the phone and going: "Sorry to laugh in your ear, but this metal seat is cold."

But, I'd never work that way — naked that is. It's unprofessional and besides, the meter reader might see me and get the wrong idea.

"I always clean up my desk before Papal visits, moon landings and whenever I change offices. But it never seems to make any difference. Try as I may, the lifelong accumulation of paper dogs my every step."

MILLENNIUM DESK CLEANING

As the next millennium approaches, I realize I have to fulfill a promise I made in my irresponsible youth — a promise to clean off my desk sometime before the turn of the next century.

While I still have a couple years to accomplish the task, I nevertheless feel a certain urgency to get started, for you see, I've attempted desk cleaning many times in the past and failed.

First of all, this is not going to be an ordinary reshuffling of papers. This is going to be a "down to the bone, everything most go, take no survivors" desk cleaning. I intend to enter the next millennium without a scrap of paper left from the 20th century sitting on my desk.

This is not to say I haven't attempted to clean my desk in the past. I always clean up my desk before Papal visits, moon landings and whenever I change offices. But it never seems to make any difference. Try as I may, the lifelong accumulation of paper dogs my every step.

Even if I move to another state the clutter follows me. This is no exaggeration. I have moved cross country, into a brand new office, in a brand new building with a brand new desk without of speck of paper anywhere in sight. Then I step out for a minute and when I return every piece of paper I have ever touched has returned to cover every inch of desk, furniture and floor space in the new office.

Everything must go....almost

So this time everything must go, including my collection of desk blotter calendars from 1975 through 1997 that I have meticulously preserved over the years, inserting each new year over the top of the last year until my blotter stands two inches above the rest of my desk.

Out will also go every unread magazine, newspaper clipping, and company procedures manual I've kept for the past two decades. With them will be trashed file folders filled with important papers I wanted to save but haven't looked at since the leisure suit was in style.

Actually, there are good reasons why I've saved most of this stuff. The number one reason is that I'm afraid to throw anything away. I just know if I toss out anything it will turn out to be something really important that I'll need someday. In fact, it never seems to fail that whenever I toss away even the most meaningless scrap of paper that I've saved for the past 10 years, the very next day my boss will call me up and say: "You know that meaningless scrap of paper you've had on your desk for 10 years. Well, I need it immediately. The fate of the free world depends on it."

I will not worry about that happening this time. This time everything will go, even the stuff inside the folders in my filing cabinets. And the honest truth is I don't have a clue what's in those folders. You see, early on in my career I learned I was not a file folder type of person. Anything I place inside a folder is lost forever. Items I have placed in folders in my file drawers might just as well have fallen into the fourth dimension. They are never seen again. So I keep everything I need on my desk. If I put anything away, it ceases to exist in my mind.

Method in the madness

Over the years, I have developed a desktop filing system that allows me to find anything I need amid a mountain of paper so high it could keep a troop of Boy Scouts at a paper drive happy for months. It's a very simple system for keeping track of stuff, and always works unless I really need to find something.

For example, the 6-inch-high stack of papers to the left of my computer is things I have to do today. The 8-inch stack of stuff to the right of my computer is tomorrow's work. The teetering load of trash on top the computer is work-in-progress, and the really urgent stuff, I keep in my lap.

On the edge of my desk stands a seven-level "In" basket filled with things that never got "Out." What's really surprising is that no one has ever asked me for any of this stuff in all the time it's been sitting there — and some of it's marked "Urgent." I keep it there because I know if I throw anything out, NATO might collapse.

But this time, no matter what the consequences, everything gets thrown out. I will be ruthless in my objective to produce a clean desk. I pledge this time, not a scrap of paper will survive.

The first pile I pick up has a grocery list on top dated Nov. 7, 1983. Out it goes without a backwards glance. Underneath is a 4-inch bundle of scrap paper I've kept for writing notes. I hesitate. "I might still need to make notes in the next millennium," I reason, then set the scrap paper aside.

Farther down is a pamphlet on "How to create a paperless office." I better keep that one for future reference in maintaining my totally clean desk.

Somewhere down in the stack, between birthday and Christmas cards and other treasured mementos I have to save, is the Owner's Guide to a 1973 Dodge Dart I once owned. "Hey, that could be a collector's item some day. I'll just store it for a while longer."

The next batch of paper floors me. It's my draft notice from President Richard Nixon. I guess he really didn't need me or he would have called. Next to it I found a half-filled book of Green Stamps. I wonder if they still redeem those things. I'll just put that over here for now and get back to them. Moments later I find my cute desk sign: "A clean desk is the work of a sick mind." I better pin that one on the wall.

After three hours of diligent work, I have managed to move everything from the top of one pile to the bottom of another and shift every bit of junk from the right side of my desk over to the left side without discarding hardly anything. The only things I've thrown out are an old grocery list and some used cellophane paper. As I ponder the uselessness of my efforts, the telephone rings. It's my boss. "Do you still have that old grocery list you've kept for the past 14 years? Bring it in, I need it right away. Also, bring along any used cellophane paper you've got."

See why I don't throw anything away?

"We want a house on the water when we retire, but our financial advisors say with our investment situation we may have to lower our expectations a little and live in a pup tent in the Florida Everglades."

SLAVING FOR RETIREMENT

Financial advisors have recently started counseling us baby boomers that we will need at least $1 million for retirement. And they keep doing it with a straight face, which leads me to believe they might be serious about this.

They actually recommend couples accumulate a nest egg of $1.5 million, especially if you want to eat out once in a while and keep gas in the car. These financial gurus estimate the average couple will need to be millionaires to retire in the next two decades just to sustain the pathetic standard of living they've got today.

Based on what my wife, Madeline, and I have managed to put away for retirement, I think we will be able to live comfortably for 10 to 15 weeks after we retire, that is if we don't have to neuter the cat or use electricity.

Talking with my financial advisors "Flywheel, Flywheel and Shyster," they recommend at our age (which is getting up there) my wife and I should be putting away about one-third of our income every month. Can you believe that, put a third into investments? I protested that the IRS is already taking a third, and if we put another third of our salaries away for retirement, we'd be living below the poverty line of a couple of gerbils.

You see, our dream has always been to retire to a house on the water where it's warm. The financial advisors, however, said with our investment situation we may have to lower our expectations a little. They said, "We think you'll be looking at a pup tent in the Florida Everglades."

Getting a jump on stocks

The current thinking of the financial community is that people should get involved in buying stocks early in life — like after high school. Stock brokers now talk about kids as young as 12 years old making investments.

Hey, I was in the market when I was 12. I regularly bought Pepsi and General Foods — I'd buy a soda and a bag of chips and I was happy.

In hindsight, I should have gotten involved in mutual funds years ago.

My problem was I thought they were saying "mutual funs," and I didn't see any point in giving my money to someone else so they could have fun with it. I knew if they had my money, there wasn't going to be any "mutual fun" in my house.

My financial advisor now says that to catch up, I should study the stock market pages of my local newspaper for aggressive growth stocks to attain my goals. Right. At my age I can barely read the regular type in the newspaper, let alone that little, tiny print they use for stock quotations. I swear, that stuff looks like Sanskrit to me.

Besides, every time I've invested heavy in the stock market, it's dropped like a rock. Remember the crash of 1987? I did that.

Part of the problem is I've never really understood the stock market. Whenever stock brokers would talk about the Bears and the Bulls I just assumed they were referring to Chicago sports teams, although I always wondered why the Cubs and White Sox were never mentioned.

Dow Jones batting averages

Face it, stocks and bonds are confusing. There's just too much you have to know about the language and terms of the stock market to be any good at it. For years, I didn't understand that Nasdaq was a stock exchange. I thought it was an economy car put out by Honda Motors. I also assumed Small Cap stocks referred to miniature hat companies. And I thought the Dow Jones Averages were batting averages of a couple of guys on the Tigers' farm team.

I never invested in hog futures, because I figured most hogs were going to wind up as sausage anyway and didn't have much of a future. And if you'd have asked me about the "Bond Index," I would have probably said it's a new James Bond movie.

On top of all this confusing language you have to learn, you also get confusing advice from brokers. One broker tells you to buy blue chips, another says get computer chips, a third says casino stocks will put you in the chips. And here I am, usually at a loss on what's the best buy in potato chips.

But my financial wizards, in addition to having me invest in stocks, are also recommending that I: 1) establish a retirement plan, 2) defer earnings to the future, 3) look at annuities and 4) buy lots of lottery tickets.

Using this advice, I set out my retirement plan expectations. I want to retire and live in Tahiti with dozens of beautiful island girls reading me the stock reports. Both my financial advisor and my wife vetoed that one, even though I thought it was a very mature and responsible plan I had devised.

Instead, the financial people suggested that we put off major purchases like a house, car, and shoes until the comet Hale-Bopp returns in about 4,000 years. That, they said, would give us a start on a sound financial pain, I mean plan.

As to deferring earnings into the future, I've already done that in a way. I've got credit card bills that will probably take us well into the next century to pay off. I also looked at annuities and I can report they are quite nice, tending towards the pastel shades.

My only hope is the lottery. That or becoming an NBA All Star basketball player, both of which pay about the same.

"Perhaps I've watched too many episodes of "Twilight Zone" in my youth, but I believe machines have an evil streak in them. Anyone who has ever tried to use one of those vending machines that "accepts" dollar bills knows what I mean."

FEAR OF THE EVIL MACHINE

The other day a local financial institution sent me an offer to try their new ATM card, which they said would give me money at more than 65,000 Automated Teller Machines world-wide.

What a wonderful offer, I thought, free money anywhere in the world. I must live right.

Then I read the small print that said I needed to have money in that bank to take money out. What a bummer.

Actually, I don't know why I even considered the offer. You see, I am one of the few remaining people on earth who does not use an ATM card. In fact, I intend to be the last person on earth to use one.

Why am I against such a supposedly efficient, modern convenience like ATMs, used by a gazillion people world-wide?

Well, number one, I have this fear of having to deal with machines on a personal basis. Especially ones that have control over my money.

Perhaps I've watched too many episodes of "Twilight Zone" in my youth, but I believe machines have an evil streak in them. Anyone who has ever tried to use one of those vending machines that "accepts" dollar bills knows what I mean.

The operative word here is "accepts," which in machine language means "Ha ha ha ha ha ha ha."

Machine rejection

Here's how they usually works: You put in your dollar bill and the machine whirls and hums and then spits back your money like it's made of moldy cheese. You look at your perfectly good dollar bill and wonder what you've done in your life to have a machine reject your simple need for a Coke and a few M&Ms.

I don't use these machines any more. I prefer to waddle around town with five pounds of change in my pockets.

The second reason I won't use ATMs is that I know someday some-one is going to figure out that those little computer screens on ATMs are really tiny TV sets and they'll start selling advertising on them.

That's just what I need when I'm at a walk-up ATM, standing out in the rain, the snow and the sleet — your typical Michigan spring day — and this machine gives me a 30-second commercial on drinking an "ice cold Pepsi."

When you get right down to it, though, I guess I'm just one of those old-fashioned people who like personal service.

I like to have the personal touch of a real live teller who knows my name and gives me change for a vending machine that has laughed at my paper money. Also, with a teller, you get free smiles, human con-tact and sometimes candy — a few of the things an ATM can never provide.

But, I haven't always felt this way about ATMs.

Using the "mad" money machines

To be perfectly truthful, I actually used an ATM machine for a month in my misbegotten youth when these demons first came out. They didn't call them ATMs in those days. They were called Money Machines, Instant Cash, and also Wall of Fortune, Shop till You Drop 'Cause You Only Live Once, and Go Out and Spend It All While You Can money convenience machines.

My company put one in next to my desk at work and once I learned to use my money card, I was like Homer Simpson. "Yaahoo, look at this dumb machine. You just put in your card, tell it you want money and it gives it to you. What a dumb machine."

It was like having my own personal slot machine that paid off ev-ery time I played it.

After the first month of using the Money Machine, I had to liqui-date my Christmas savings account, cancel my kids' college fund and put off neutering the dog to pay off my bills. The next day I cut up my money card with its secret PIN and never looked back.

Nevertheless, I have to admit I was attracted to the allure of the new bank card I was offered. It said I could use it anywhere in the world to get money. Considering I've spent most of my adult life within about 15 miles of my house, I somehow found this idea strangely ap-pealing.

I do travel, I reasoned. I do go to Sludge Hollow once in a while. Having the security to know that I had a piece of plastic in my pocket that would give me untold riches —up to my daily limit — had its advantages.

But then I began to wonder about what in the world I would need that money for anyway? I couldn't think of a single thing I would need cash for that I couldn't just pay for with a check.

Well actually, I did think of one thing. If I were getting robbed, for instance, and the hold-up guy wouldn't take a check, I might need to have cash.

In the end, I decided not to get the bank card. I couldn't see getting an ATM card on the off-chance I might get mugged some day in Sludge Hollow.

This is a blank page. I forgot what I was going to put here, so use this space for your own memories.

Chapter II

CLONED SHEEP ARE A BAAAD JOKE

Scientists should forget about cloning barnyard animals and stick to important issues like making handy garden gadgets and automatic toilet paper refillers. Maybe they could even get my car to run.

I won't go into the exact description of how they cloned a sheep, but it sounds like a lot more work than, say, just putting two sheep together and leaving them alone for a while with some romantic music and soft lighting.

CLONED SHEEP ARE A BAAAD JOKE

I don't know if you heard about it, but some Scottish scientists claim they've cloned a sheep.

When I first read the story, I thought it was just a baaaad joke. I mean, having a Scotsman cloning sheep is like having an Iowa farmer claim he's cloned wheat.

"Yep, that wheat field I cloned is exactly like the other one over there, and that one over that, and that one..." says farmer Brown.

And like wheat, it's kind of hard to spot the differences between sheep. They all look alike to me. Even sheep sometimes have a hard time telling themselves apart. You can often hear sheep asking each other: "Is that ewe, you, or is ewe, me?"

I won't go into the exact description of how they cloned a sheep, but it sounds like a lot more work than, say, just putting two sheep together and leaving them alone for a while with some romantic music and soft lighting.

But everybody's making a big deal out of it. The sheep, whose name is Dolly, has gotten its picture in the *New York Times* and in a bunch of major magazines. Even *People* magazine is considering doing a personality piece on it, if they can figure out how to get the sheep into a picture with Brad Pitt.

Laughing up their kilts

Actually, I think those Scotsmen are laughing up their kilts at us right now. For one, I've seen "Braveheart," and I don't think they're technologically advanced enough to do this kind of thing. I think the whole cloning thing is a hoax and they'll need more than identical DNA from two different sheep to convince me. Hey, I'm sure the O.J. defense team could prove the DNA's not exactly alike and that Det. Mark Fuhrman planted the second sheep.

What's got everybody worked up about this is that now it might be possible to clone human beings.

Basketball fanatics are already talking about the possibility of cloning basketball superstars Michael Jordan and Shaquille O'Neill and making whole teams of their genetic duplicates.

I think what they forget is that basketball has changed dramatically during the past 25 years and will probably change even more in the future. By the time the replicated Jordans and Shaqs hit the courts in 20 years the average basketball player will probably be nine feet tall, have three arms, and tackling will be allowed. Up against those kind of players, the duplicates of Jordan and O'Neill would probably be lucky to get 18 maybe 20 points a game, max.

Cloning and the IRS

The moral issue of cloning humans also has come to the forefront since Dolly the sheep made her appearance. One of the key questions society has to deal with is whether cloning will make all those government forms that ask for the names of your mother and father obsolete.

Cloning yourself could be very hard on the Internal Revenue Service, especially if people start putting down their dependents as "Me, Me, and Me."

The President has already named an advisory panel of ethical experts to consider limitations on human cloning. So far, though, all they've come up with is that no one will be allowed to clone Dennis Rodman.

"The mechanical problems my cars develop are always things that cost half as much as the Federal Deficit to fix. It really irks me when those mechanics start pulling out the travel brochures as I drive in for repairs."

'HOUSTON, WE HAVE A CAR PROBLEM'

What is it with cars these days? They get a few decades old and start breaking down all the time.

I've got three cars — well, four if you count the rusting Volvo in the drive that has become a home to woodland creatures — and they're always breaking down on me. It seems like the only place I drive to these days has hydraulic lifts and the word "repair" in its name.

And the mechanical problems my cars develop are always things that cost half as much as the Federal Deficit to fix. It really irks me when those mechanics start pulling out the travel brochures as I drive in for repairs. I swear my last three mechanics have all retired to the South of France to condos on the Riviera. What's worse is when they send me those post cards that read "Wish you were here, we're getting low on funds."

If you're wondering why I have so many cars the reason is simple. I have four cars so I have one to drive while the other three are in the repair shop. I tell you, my mechanical woes have gotten so bad that tow truck drivers follow me around town whenever they feel lucky.

My own car is like the Mir Space Station. It seems to break down every other day. The most recent spat of repairs started a few weeks ago when my wife tried to dock it with the garage and put a 10-foot gash in the side. The repair estimate came in at like $2 million, so I filled the crease with some gum and covered it with spray paint just like they do with the real Mir Space Station.

A galaxy of trouble

Anyway, the week the Russians were having control problems with their space station, I was driving back from the grocery store when my on-board computer went out and the car began to wobble uncontrollably all over the road. I had to shut down the life support systems — the radio and air conditioner — and jettison the groceries to bring it back under control.

As bad as this car runs, I've still had several offers from people to buy it. In fact, the Russians want it for spare parts for their space program.

Actually, it's very suspicious sometimes how these car problems occur. For instance, I'll take my car in because the left turn signal doesn't work and the garage discovers they have to replace my entire electrical system to fix it. I get that done and the turn signal still doesn't work, and neither does my horn.

Unable to find the problem with the horn, the garage rigs up this string tied to the tail of a cat that howls whenever I pull the string. It's not a perfect system but it is economical. I get about 100 miles to a box of Meow Mix and the cat sticks her paw out the side of the engine whenever I have to make left turns.

Mine is not the only car I have problems with. My wife's car also has something wrong with it. It keeps running into things every time she drives it.

I've had the steering checked on her car several times and everything seemed to be working fine. The last mechanic that looked at it suggested the problem might be the on-board guidance system. I asked "what's that?" He just smiled and whispered, "That's the driver."

While her car is the most dependable of the lot even if it keeps running into things, it too has its little quirks. It keeps losing body parts in our driveway. But these parts don't seem to fit anywhere or affect the operation of the car.

Every week, I find nuts, bolts and strangely shaped pieces of twisted metal lying around her car that don't seem to have any purpose or function. Last week I found a section of car frame under the front fender. I took it to the body shop and they couldn't find any place it might go on the car. "Actually," said the repair man, "it looks like it came off a 1989 Buick. You hit anything lately?"

Finding a car for the kids

My oldest son has a car that only has two gears out of five that work. The problem is it's never the same two gears. Sometimes it's first and reverse that work and sometimes it's just park and neutral. The interesting thing is that whenever it runs right, it's "his" car, but when it breaks, it's "Dad's" car.

I shouldn't really complain about the cars my kids drive because I'm the one that picks them out. We'll go to the auto graveyard and they'll be looking at some flashy red sports car, while I'm looking for something Fred Flintstone might have driven. I like to buy my teenage drivers the biggest and slowest cars I can find for their safety and protection.

My favorite was a 1981 Oldsmobile that could go from 0 to 50 in an hour and a half if you really punched it. The best feature of the car was its "underdrive" system. If you were going along the highway at 55 mph and you stepped on the gas real hard, the car would slow down. It was a perfect feature for teenagers, even though my kids kept begging me to get it fixed. If I could have figured out how it worked, I would have taken out a patent on it and sold it to parents of other teenage drivers.

It's all where you shop

A friend of mine suggested my car problems might have something to do with where I buy my cars. I said he was wrong and hotly defended the integrity of "Fred and Bubba's Abandoned Car Lot."

"They always treat me like a king whenever I go in there," I said, recalling the time they broke open the champagne when they saw me walk in the door.

Fred and Bubba have never steered me wrong. For example, they said I'd never need any anti-theft devices on any cars I bought from them because no one would ever want to steal them. But I didn't believe them when I bought my last car there, a vintage 1990 Yugo. I went out and got myself "The Club," an anti-theft steel bar that locks your steering wheel in place so no one can take your car. It's a good thing I did that, too, because the first time I parked the Yugo downtown someone broke into it. Luckily, the only thing they stole was "The Club."

I'm beginning to think I'm just unlucky at buying cars. They all look good and run great in the used car lot, and then they start breaking down the instant my 30-second or three-mile warranty expires.

I remember one car I bought, a low-mileage, used 1969 Rambler —yes I've owned classic cars before — that broke down the day after I bought it. I took it to the repair shop and they found the problem immediately. The squirrel in the cage that powered the car had died. I replaced him with two new squirrels and a family of gerbils, but I still had problems with the car. I finally realized why the car had such low mileage. It never left my garage.

I tried to unload it on some other unsuspecting buyers, but no one would even take it for a "test sit" in my driveway. I finally was able to sell the car one day when the "R" in RAMBLER fell off the front of the hood.

I advertised it as a new, German-engineered car called the "AMBLER" and it sold right away. Actually, if anyone's in the market to buy a car right now, I've got this yard full of European-engineered autos like the UGO, OLVO and MIR that I'll let you have real cheap.

"I have every garden tool ever invented. Why do I have all of this stuff? Because it makes the yardwork easier during the one hour a week I spend puttering around outside."

A UNIVERSAL GARDEN TOOL CAN SAVE MY LIFE

What this country needs is a good multi-purpose, snow-blowing, leaf-sucking, grass-cutting, riding rototiller and sidewalk edger. If such a thing could be invented, I would be the first in line to buy one. Then I could get all of these other yard machines and garden tools out of my garage to make room for things like my car. It might even save my life.

I wonder sometimes where all of this stuff comes from and why today the average homeowner feels they need to have as much lawn and garden equipment as a landscaping company.

When I was growing up, my dad did all of the yard work with a shovel, a rake and a foot-powered grass cutter. With those three implements, he kept our yard in perfect shape through the four seasons of the year.

With the shovel, he tilled the garden, edged the walkways, built patios and landscaped the yard. In the winter, he wielded the shovel to dig us out of the snow and put coal in the furnace. The rake was used to pile up leaves in fall, thatch the lawn in spring, weed the garden in summer and keep the shed door closed year-round. The grass cutter simply cut the grass. That's all it had to do in those days; the shovel and rake did all the rest.

Wayward shrubs

If there were any other yard implements he needed to tend the grass, garden and flower beds, my father would find a solution with the tools at hand. Once, at my mother's insistence, we planted bushes around the sides of the house. When they started growing, my dad discovered he'd have to get hedge cutters to keep them trimmed. That's what any other person would do, but not my dad. Buying hedge clippers would involve putting another nail into the garden shed wall to hang it on. And, that would throw off the symmetry of the carefully arranged grass cutter, shovel and rake that hung there already.

So instead of buying hedge clippers, he simply sharpened one side of the shovel and hacked away at the offending bushes until they were chopped into submission and more or less even. When the bushes eventually got too high to do this anymore, he took the shovel one day and dug out the bushes.

Part of the reason my father could get away with so few tools was because everything in our yard and around the house was laid out in perfectly straight lines. There were no scalloped flower beds, no wandering walkways, no offending shrubbery that might require a detour with the lawn mower. Everything was laid out in perfect squares and rectangles. "It's nature's way, at this house," he liked to say.

The other reason he needed so few yard implements was that he was very creative at adapting other household items to do the job. If there was a gardening tool he didn't have, he simply improvised. He would use a claw hammer to dig shallow trenches for plantings, wield household scissors to prune the rose bushes, and dig out weeds with a screw driver. He once cut down an entire dead tree with a hacksaw. As for watering the lawn, he left that up to God.

Gotta have lawn gizmos

I, on the other hand, have to have every lawn and garden gizmo imaginable. Hanging on my garage wall are a dozen different types of rakes. I've got leaf rakes, garden rakes, lawn rakes, thatching rakes, plastic and metal rakes, plus a pile of broken rakes which I keep for spare parts. I've got tree saws, limb saws, chain saws, pruning saws, circular saws and a saw on a long pole for trimming tall tree branches. I've got snow shovels, edging shovels, trenching shovels, round hole digging shovels, square hole digging shovels, and a sharpened coal shovel from my father which I use for trimming bushes.

For the garden, I've got potting trowels, earth claws, a fence-hole digger, corn-row planter, seed dispenser, growing baskets, root massagers and an electric watering system. I've even got something called a Garden Weasel with rotating spiked wheels that I've never used because I'm afraid I'll hurt myself if I handle it wrong.

That's just the non-mechanical devices. I won't go into all the electrical and gas powered stuff I own, but suffice it to say I have a snowblower the highway department sometimes borrows to clear Interstate 196, and you get the picture.

Why do I have all of this stuff? Because it makes the yardwork easier during the one hour a week I spend puttering around outside.

But all of these energy saving tools and machines are getting out of hand. They've taken over my garage and are multiplying to point where they have become a risk to life and limb. They hang, dangle, lean and sit around every nook and cranny of my garage, resting precariously on hooks, nails, and hangers, mounted to walls, ceiling and storage racks.

I fully expect all of this stuff to come crashing down on me one of these days, and you'll read in the papers, "Man mauled by garden tools in own garage." And they'll probably quote my wife saying: "I think he would have survived if the Garden Weasel hadn't got him."

"Some seemingly perplexing questions like 'Why do socks disappear in the clothes dryer?' are easy. Clothes dryers are really doorways to an alternate dimension, and socks sometimes fall through."

SOLVING LIFE'S MYSTERIES

Scientists have recently discovered what makes coffee rings form, which is a mystery of nature that I've always wondered about.

Why does an accidentally spilled dab of coffee turn into one of those circular rings under your cup even if it starts out looking like the Blob?

The question, it seems, also perplexed heavy coffee drinkers and physics professors at the University of Chicago.

Working with gallons of decaf and regular coffee, these great minds discovered that when you spill coffee on a counter, the stain will spread out until it is trapped by microscopic rough edges on the kitchen counter.

Stuck there, the errant Brazilian blend around your coffee cup begins to evaporate at the front as it cools. The liquid behind comes up to fill in the gap for what's evaporated and a coffee ring is born.

This discovery has astounded the scientific community and the waitresses at Starbucks. While at the moment, there is no known use for the finding, i.e. it can't be turned into weapons or used as a Website on the Internet, at least now I have an answer for when my wife goes "How'd those coffee rings get on the counter?"

Science fascinates me

I've been fascinated with science from my early childhood. Well, maybe not exactly fascinated, but at least mildly interested from time-to-time. One of the things that has always intrigued me is the Mister Coffee coffee maker. If you put ten cups of water into a Mister Coffee brewer it produces nine cups of coffee. If you put in eight cups of water, you get back seven cups of coffee.

I've always wondered where that other cup of water goes. People always say the water is absorbed by the coffee grounds. But if you try to squeeze the coffee out of them, like I've done in the pursuit of science and an extra cup of coffee, nothing comes out.

Because of this, I've always held that Einstein's theory that matter in the universe can neither be created or destroyed is wrong, and the Mister Coffee makers are proof that matter can be destroyed. For years I've lived in fear that millions of us coffee brewers were unwittingly destroying the matter of our universe making it increasingly smaller, perhaps as part of some evil alien plot to conquer the galaxy.

I worried about this until I discovered rabbits. Besides being cute, and bringing us eggs at Easter, and sometimes eating all my shrubbery, rabbits serve another purpose. They keep the universe in balance.

Unlike the Mister Coffee maker which gives you less matter than you put in, if you give a cup of food to a rabbit you will get two cups of bunny droppings in return. Thus, rabbits keep the matter in the universe in constant balance, replacing whatever Mister Coffee takes away.

Unanswered questions

If we just stop and look around us, there are thousands of unanswered questions like this in our world. For example, why does the second half of a bar of soap disappear faster than the first half? And why don't soap nubs—those little pieces left after you've used all the soap—ever disappear?

Also, have you ever wondered why corn grows straight up, but ivy grows along the ground? Wouldn't this be a different world if corn grew flat and ivy went straight up?

The world is just full of such intriguing and perplexing questions, even in the business world. Just the other day I read in the newspaper that Citicorp, the nation's second-largest bank, is eliminating 7,500 employees from its customer service departments to make its customer service area "more efficient."

I tried to call Citicorp to understand their secret of doing more with less people, but I couldn't get through. All I got was an answering machine that said "Both of our customer service people are currently busy. To receive more efficient service, please hang up and don't call back."

Another bizarre phenomena of the business world is the $29.95 hotel room you see advertised all over the country. Has anyone ever found one vacant? Every time I try to get one, it's always just been rented.

Some seemingly perplexing question like "Why do socks disappear in the clothes dryer?" are easy. Clothes dryers are really doorways to an alternate dimension, and socks sometimes fall through.

Evidently I'm not the only one who is intrigued by these mysteries of the world. A reader, Paula E., writes, "When I fill ice trays with water and then go to get ice the next day, there are no ice cubes left in the tray. What happens to the ice?"

I have an answer to your question, Paula. If you had said there was only one ice cube left in each tray, then I would say your kids are using up the ice and not refilling the trays. Kids are notorious for leaving only one ice cube in the tray because then it is not completely empty and they don't have to refill it.

But since you say the trays are always empty, I think what's happening is you are putting the ice trays into the microwave oven by mistake.

Paula also writes, "Why is it that only mothers and wives seem to be the only person in the house able to notice when the toilet roll is out of paper?"

I can't answer that question, Paula. I've never noticed that problem before.

"If companies really want to be helpful, they should hook up their automated answering system to the Psychic Network. You'd call them up and they'd answer: 'Hi, this is the Psychic Answering System. We got your order telepathically.'

HELP! A REAL PERSON ANSWERED MY CALL

Something unusual happened the other day. I called up a company to check on an order I had placed and a human actually answered the phone.

I was so shocked I didn't know what to say.

"This is Very Large corporation. How can I help you?"

"Ahhhhhh," was all I could get out.

"Are you all right sir? You sound ill," said the polite voice on the other end.

Thinking I had reached a human through some electronic error, I began hitting the number keys to correct the problem. I hit the number "1" key on my phone pad, then I hit numbers "2" through "5," just like I had been trained to do by these computerized systems.

"Will you stop buzzing those numbers into my ear and tell me who you'd like to talk to," said the voice on the other end of the phone.

"Can I talk to the operator?" I asked, not knowing what else to say.

"I am the operator," said the voice. "How can I help you?"

"Ahhhhh," I said, lost for words at not only reaching a human in my first try, but also an operator. I hadn't talked to an operator in years.

"Listen," I said. "Would you mind putting me on hold for a few minutes while I gather my thoughts and write up my grocery list?"

"That's a strange request, but I'll be glad to do it," she said.

"And could you play some elevator music while I'm waiting?"

"Whatever you want," she said, sending me off to the peace and comfort of Muzak. As I listened to the elevator version of "I Can't Get No Satisfaction," I felt I was once again on familiar ground. As usual, as soon as I was on hold, my mind began to wander.

I began to think of how simple telephone answering systems were when they first came out. You only had two choices. You could wait for your party to answer, or press "0" for an operator. Now companies want to handle every possible contingency with the automated answering system, so it takes 10 minutes for the stupid machine to get to the problem you have.

Psychic system service

If companies really want to be helpful, they should hook up their automated dialing system to the Psychic Network. It would save a lot of time and energy.

You'd call them up and they'd answer: "Hi, this is the Psychic Answering System. Your order will be delivered tomorrow."

"Why that's amazing. I was just about to ask you about that package."

"Yes we know," they'd answer.

Another good idea would be for companies doing telemarketing to use the Psychic Network. No one would ever bother you with unwanted calls again. They would not only know when to call you, but know exactly what you want to buy.

"Hi, Mr. Kukla. This is the Psychic Telemarketing System and we got your order for the green sweater telepathically. For your convenience, we have upgraded it to an extra large size because we see you gaining about 20 pounds this winter.

"Also be cautious between the 14th and 21st of the month in affairs of the heart. Thank you for your business."

Now that I think about it, Psychic Telemarketing may not be such a good idea after all. Besides, I'm not going to gain 20 pounds this winter.

Two groups that should start using automated phone systems are churches and hospitals.

You could call up your favorite church and their answering machine would go: "Hello, you've reached the Church of the Good Word. To Repent, press '1.' For redemption, press '2.' To hear a repeat of Sunday's sermon, hit '3.' "

Hospitals could really streamline their systems with answering machines that handle emergencies.

"Hello. You've reached the Anemic Community Hospital. If this is an emergency involving large amounts of blood, press '1.' If this is an emergency involving broken bones, press '2.' If you have a tummy ache, press '3.' And if you have a runny nose, cold and a fever take two aspirins and call us in the morning."

Surgery by phone

Or, you might find yourself having to go in for an operation. So you call the hospital and an automated voice comes on and gives you these instructions:

"Hi, you've reached the automatic operation scheduling service. For an exploratory operation to see if there's anything wrong with you, press '1.' Gallbladder operations press '2.' Organ transplants press '3.'"

Hospitals could even have special messages for psychiatric patients. "If you're having paranoid delusions, put down the knife and press '1.' Individuals with compulsive disorders press '2, eleven times.' Those with multiple personalities press '3,' '4,' '5' and '6.' "

My revelry was brought to an end when the operator came back on the line and said "Very Large Corporation, can I help you now?"

"I have to apologize about my behavior earlier," I said. "Hearing a real person answer a phone at a business was a rather strange and unique experience for me. You don't usually find that kind of service any more in a large corporation."

She thanked me and said that was part of their company's customer- service policy.

"We like to give everyone VIP treatment," she said. "Now who would you like to speak to?"

"I'd like to talk to Bill Smith in order processing."

"I'll connect you now," she said. The phone rang and Bill Smith came on the line.

"Hi, this is Bill Smith. I'm not in right now, but if you'd like to leave a voice message press '1.' If you want to send me a fax press '2.' If you'd like to be connected to the Psychic Network press '3.' "

Chapter III

TOO MUCH PASTA IS NEVER ENOUGH

I like my pasta just like my women -- covered in tomato sauce and garnished with lots of cheese. Oops, bad analogy, I meant hot and firm. No, forget that too. This chapter is about food.

"Over the years my family has come to accept my little character flaw and live with it. But above all, God bless them, they've learned how to eat huge quantities of leftover pasta."

TOO MUCH PASTA IS NEVER ENOUGH

I've had a secret problem for years that only my immediate family knows about.

The problem is too horrible to mention, but I'll tell you about it anyway. I overcook spaghetti. When I say I overcook spaghetti, I don't mean I cook it too long. What dolt would do that? I mean I cook too much.

Actually, that is a gross understatement. I made so much spaghetti once, we had to store the excess in the bathtub. What a mess that was. Have you ever tried to put Saran Wrap on a bathtub?

Over the years my family has come to accept my little character flaw and live with it. But above all, God bless them, they've learned how to eat huge quantities of leftover pasta. What that means is that weeks after I cook Italian, our diet consists of nothing but spaghetti sandwiches, rigatoni omelettes and deep fried lasagna on a stick. I have no shame. I will fill their lunch bags with macaroni and pasta pitas until we get rid of the stuff.

To let you know how bad this problem is, I once stuffed our Thanksgiving turkey with medium shells left over from a Halloween party we threw. We have a linguine-loving Chihuahua that weighs 100 pounds, and in winter I leave bowls of cooked spaghetti on my neighbors' doorsteps with unsigned notes that read "Just thinking of you."

Falling off the pasta wagon

During the past year I've managed to stay away from the kitchen stove and the boxes of uncooked, tricolor, penne pasta that keep calling to me from the cupboards. But I broke down the other day.

We were having company for dinner and I thought I would surprise my wife, Madeline, by having the pasta ready when she got home from work.

I started out by judiciously taking out a single, one-pound package of Angel Hair pasta for our repast. As I unwrapped the slender stalks of golden grain and hefted it in my hand, I thought to myself, "That's not enough spaghetti to feed a hungry family of field mice, let alone four mature adults." So I took out two hefty boxes of No. 9 semolina thick strands and dumped that into the boiling water instead. But it still didn't look like enough, so I threw in the Angel Hair stuff for good measure.

As the water boiled, my brain said "enough already" but my hands kept adding more.

"Everyone loves pasta," I said, tossing in a half-used box of linguine that was just sitting around. And in case that wasn't enough, I added some spinach and pepper noodles for color.

When my wife got home that night, huge, brimming bowls of steaming pasta covered every inch of the kitchen. Dozens of larger bowls sat on the dining room table and sideboard, spilling their contents onto the floor.

"Surprise," I said. "I cooked the pasta."

She was so happy, she was speechless. Almost in a trance she staggered around the kitchen clutching at her chest, her joy was so great.

"Tell me a spaghetti factory exploded," she said. "Tell me we've won the Publisher's Clearinghouse Sweepstake and they're paying us off in cooked spaghetti. Tell me we've been invaded by the Italian Army. But don't tell me you've been cooking pasta again."

"Well, I might have gotten a little carried away," I admitted as she opened the refrigerator and a plastic garbage bag of fusilli spirals slithered out.

"Who's going to eat all of this stuff?" she asked, sitting down on one of the kitchen chairs just as I pulled a spaghetti bowl out from under her.

"So we have some leftovers. Everybody loves reheated spaghetti," I suggested. "Besides, we're having guests for dinner and we can always send a few barrels home with them."

The traumatic linguine incident

Over the years I've tried to figure out why I have this urge to cook more pasta than can be eaten by the Detroit Lions in five or six days. Once or twice I've tried to kick the habit by joining Pasta Overcookers Anonymous and going to the Betty Fettuccine Clinic, but nothing worked.

After the last incident, though, my wife said I needed professional help and sent me to a psychologist and best-selling pasta cookbook author, Dr. Al Dente.

But I thought he was a little tough on me. He said my problem came from infancy.

"When you were a baby, your mother probably dropped you on your noodle," he said, chuckling.

"I'm sorry," said Dr. Dente, wiping tears from his eyes. "I just couldn't resist that one."

Actually, my problem is not that uncommon he said. Many people evidently suffer from this same inability to measure spaghetti correctly. The disease even has a name. It's called "Lackalinguinephobia." Or, explaining it in layman's terms, he said I was "a few strands short of a full bowl."

We discovered (over several bowls of leftover spaghetti I brought along with me to his office) that in my early childhood I had a traumatic experience with spaghetti that I sublimated from my conscious self.

Cub Master Bob makes dinner

It seems that when I was about eight years old, I went on an overnight camping trip with the Cub Scouts. After we had pitched our little tents and gathered up wood for the campfire, our leader, Cub Master Bob, announced we would be having spaghetti for dinner.

As we opened the cans of tomato sauce, Cub Master Bob began putting the spaghetti into a big cooking pot full of boiling water.

"I figure there's 15 of us, so we should be able to eat about a pound, a pound and a half each," he said, dumping 23 pounds of uncooked, assorted pasta into the pot. Obviously, he too suffered from an advanced case of Lackalinguinephobia.

In about 20 minutes, the lid of the pot popped off and this yellow mass of simmering goo began climbing out. It crawled out of the pot and started making its way across the dirt ground towards us, as we huddled behind Cub Master Bob.

"Don't fear men, I've never lost a Scout to pasta yet," he said, brandishing a ladle at the advancing wall of noodles.

As we watched in horror, a long arm of lasagna whipped out of the boiling mass and grabbed the ladle from his hand.

"It's gone berserk. Run for your lives," he yelled as 14 Cub Scouts and their leader ran screaming in terror across the campground, pursued by a mammoth blob of seething pasta.

Instead of running with the pack, I dived into my tent for shelter. It was a mistake. The blob followed me in, moving toward me in a slithering mass. As I huddled in the back of the tent, I realized there was no way out. I was going to become a side dish to the pasta monster.

I was trapped. So I did the only thing I could. I pulled out my Scout knife and opened it to the fork and began eating my way to freedom.

They found me a few hours later, unconscious in a pool of marinara sauce. The doctor who checked me out said I had the worst case of indigestion he'd ever seen, but otherwise I was fine.

I thought I would be cured of my obsession once I had this knowledge, but one thing still bothered me. If I had been traumatized by this incident, why would I repeatedly make larger and larger quantities of pasta?

Dr. Dente said I continually overcooked pasta now because I was still trying to recreate and control this traumatic experience from my youth.

"It's either that or you're just a lousy cook," he said.

*"When I was growing up in the 1950s, potatoes were a
staple of one or more meals a day at our house.
It was part of your four basic food groups —
meat, vegetables, dairy products and potatoes."*

THIS "SPUD'S" FOR YOU

I sent my son out the other night for some groceries for dinner, and potatoes were on the list. Since I didn't specify that I wanted real, from the earth, still-in-the-skins potatoes, he brought home these four frozen potato halves that cost $4.99.

I was dumbfounded. Who in their right mind would pay $4.99 for the equivalent of two split potatoes with a little fake cheese sprinkled on top? Then I realized I had.

Now, I'm not one to stand in the way of culinary advancements in easy-to-prepare foods, but really, how much effort does to take to split a potato in half, nuke it for 10 minutes or so — 30 seconds extra if you want to melt a Kraft American cheese slice on top — and serve?

I was just glad, though, that my mother wasn't there looking over my shoulder to see this potato extravagance my son had brought home. I know exactly what she would say: "You paid $5 for two potatoes. I used to feed a family of four for a week on that."

And she did. There was no one who could stretch a food budget like my mom. And she did it with potatoes.

When I was growing up in the 1950s, potatoes were a staple of one or more meals a day at our house. It was part of your four basic food groups — meat, vegetables, dairy products and potatoes.

What potato famine?

We had fried potatoes, baked potatoes, twice baked, Au grautin, scalloped, mashed, boiled, and hashed. She'd make American fries, French fries, home fries, skillet fries, and julienne fries. Potatoes were browned in a roaster, fried in pan, baked in an oven, simmered in a pot of butter and wrapped in tinfoil and cooked on the grill.

When my brother and I were growing up, it was bulk that counted. My brother in those days, and still today, would eat shoe leather if someone else prepared it and it came with French fries and ketchup. His favorite meal is still whole potatoes in the skin, blackened in an open fire until there's a half inch of charcoal surrounding the potato. "Man that's good eatin'," he would say, charcoal chunks falling from his mouth.

Potatoes were the bulk that sustained us from meal-to-meal, day-to-day, week-to-week. My mother could actually make a whole meal out of nothing but potatoes. Well, that might be a slight exaggeration, but not by much. She could take a bowl of mashed potatoes, blend it with flour and water, rough it into potato dough and turn the result into intriguing and exotic pasta dishes.

Don't get me wrong, we had other things besides potatoes. We'd have a roast on Sunday, which became hash on Tuesday, a couple meals with hamburger during the week and of course pork chops on Saturday. Steaks were for birthdays. Turkey for Thanksgiving. Ham for Christmas and Easter.

Vegetables flourished in summer

Fresh vegetables were a summer food, planted in backyard gardens during the spring and eaten in mass quantities while they flourished in the heat of summer. The surplus of what we didn't eat was canned in Mason jars for storage and consumption during the fall and winter.

Dairy products, if you can believe it, were delivered to the house by milkmen, along with butter, cheese, eggs and even fruit juice. There was no running out every-other-day to the convenience store for milk. It just miraculously appeared every morning on your doorstep.

On the other hand, nobody delivered potatoes; you had to go out and search them out for yourself.

Every fall my mother and father would scour the country farms in search of the largest, heartiest, most economical potatoes they could find. It wasn't unusual for them to come back with one hundred and fifty pounds of potatoes for winter use. At $5 a bushel, I might add.

They brought them home in bags, boxes and sacks, sorted them by size — small, medium and large — and stored them in baskets and bins along the walls of our old fruit cellar, from which we would consume them one-by-one during the long winter.

The Friday French fry feast

Friday lunches were always my favorite when I was growing up. Those were the days when Catholics didn't eat meat on Friday so we had to be creative with our meals, otherwise you wound up eating fish and tomato soup all the time. I can remember coming home for lunch on cold February Fridays to an entire plate of hot and crispy French fries my mother had made us for lunch.

These weren't your ordinary fast-food French fries, that travesty of reconstituted potato muck, shaped expertly to one-quarter inch diameter, so they can fit upright in little paper sacks. No, these were real French fries my mother made. French fries that were big and hearty like the earthy spud they sprang from. They were a half-inch thick and cooked to a crisp golden brown on the outside, served dripping with oil, with a center soft and hot to the tongue. I'd eat them slathered with ketchup and salt, or if I was daring, with vinegar and ketchup.

Unfortunately, those days are gone, knocked off and nearly forgotten by fast-food franchised potato sticks and our desire for quick no fuss meals. That and the fact that hot, grease-dripping French fries aren't healthy for you anyway. I think they were banned by the federal government in the Saturated Fat and Cholesterol Act of 1994, but I still dream of them even today from time-to-time.

In fact, as I was putting away the groceries my son had brought home, in one of the plastic sacks I came across a bag of thick-cut, half-inch diameter, frozen Idaho French fries. I looked at them for a moment and my mouth began to water. Oh well, I guess you can't stop progress. Now where's the oil. Give me the vinegar. Bring on the ketchup and let's feast.

"Fred and Bubba's Shop & Bag had slipped into the Twilight Zone and come out the other side turned into a weird upscale supermarketeria and gastronomic food entertainment center where Mariachi bands played. ❧

FRED AND BUBBA'S GONE UPSCALE

My wife and I went to Fred and Bubba's Shop & Bag the other night to pick up some franks and beans for dinner.

I knew something was wrong the minute I walked into the grocery store. Instead of the usual mass of banged-up and rusting grocery carts lining the front door, there was now a wall of shrubs and potted plants decorating the entrance. Behind a podium among the plants stood a tuxedoed maitre' d waiting to greet us.

"Ah, you are just in time for dinner. I have a beautiful table for two in our dining room near the window," he said, picking up a couple of menus and beckoning us to follow him.

"We have a fine veal scallopini tonight. It's a specialty of zee chef, served in a light wine sauce," he said, kissing his fingertips.

"I'm sorry. I think there's been a mistake," I said. "We were looking for Fred and Bubba's Shop & Bag and must have wandered into your fashionable restaurant by mistake."

"Oh, you make zee little joke," he said. "This ees the new Fred and Bubba's supermarketeria and gastronomic food entertainment center."

"Look, we didn't come here to be entertained," I said, as a Mariachi band began playing in the frozen food aisle. "We want the place where you buy bags of grub and then take it home and eat it," I explained.

Searching out the "cart steward"

"Ah, my mistake, sir," he apologized. "You want to dine a la cart tonight. I shall get the 'cart' steward to assist you immediately."

While he went off to summon the cart steward, I turned to my wife to find out what the heck was going on, but she had wandered off to the florist shop nearby and was consulting with the botanist there on the design for a greenhouse we might want to install at our home.

"Don't look now," I said, pulling her to the side, "but I think we've stumbled into the Twilight Zone.

"I believe we have entered a dimension of sight and sound similar to our own, but strangely different," I said, looking around for the grocery store that had once stocked corn dogs, Cheese Whiz and Chef Boyardee canned ravioli. All of that great stuff had been replaced by designer pizzas, tomato-bisque bagels and something called "hummus."

"Let's just casually head for the door and make a break for it when no one is looking," I said, trying to drag her away from a brand new Sushi Bar that now occupied the space where I used to buy slightly dented canned goods.

"Don't be silly," she said. "This is our old supermarket. They just updated it and added a few new things."

"Oh yeah. If that's true, then where's Ralph the bag boy," I challenged.

"He's been promoted," she said pointing to someone who had the same pear-shaped body as Ralph, but who now looked almost distinguished, decked out in the traditional whites of a pastry chef.

"He's the new pastry consultant," she explained. "Ralph advises people what styles of bread, muffins and dinner rolls will go best with their kitchen decor."

I had to admit it looked like Ralph, but he somehow appeared different. He looked — how can I say this — clean. "Oh, poor Ralph, they've taken his body and made a pod-person out of him," I muttered to myself.

Which way to the disco?

"Look dear," my wife said, ignoring my anguished expression. "I've got to pick up a few things over in Produceland. Why don't we meet later at the store's espresso bar and disco? We'll talk," she said, giving me air kisses on both cheeks.

After she left, I wandered aimlessly through the new store.

The place was huge and it had everything you could image. There was a wine cellar, a pharmaceutical boutique, and a butcher shop the size of Cleveland. There was a newsstand, delicatessen, shoe store and a small-scale Disneyland for the kids. They had valet parking and in-cart movies, a lending library, dentist office and bank. There was even a championship golf course with a lake just across from the new, 24-screen cineplex.

All this place needed was some hotel rooms and I could have booked us in for our next vacation.

While other shopping "guests" ambled through the store marveling at the wondrous and fashionable decor, I went into a state of shock. Somewhere, somehow, my favorite grocery store had become upscale. I felt like I had lost an old friend.

All of the familiar landmarks I had come to associate with grocery shopping — like aisles one through ten — had disappeared and been replaced with cutesy neighborhoods named "Pasta Village," "Ye Ol' Bagel Way" and a chicken parts repository called "Chez Poulet."

"This can't be happening," I cried aloud, my head swimming from the aroma of fresh baked zitti in aged Parmesan cheese which a Julia Childs' android was whipping up at one of the demonstration cooking booths.

"Where's the Spam?" I shouted, knocking over a tray of grilled salmon and caper appetizers being offered by a Martha Stewart clone.

"Where's my Hostess Ding Dongs and Little Debbie Snacks?" I blubbered as I ran blindly from one trendy aisle to the next, searching in vain for the staples of life.

"Man cannot live by Chicken Caesar Salad alone," I cried, running in horror from an in-store salad bar that would have humbled the great chefs of the Ponderosa Steakhouse.

Lost in the land of hummus

My wife found me in Seafood City holding off the souse chef with a package of frozen swordfish, as I demanded to know where all the fish sticks had been taken.

"There, there dear. It's okay. You'll be just fine," she said gently, leading me away.

"But you don't understand," I whimpered. "They've taken Mrs. Paul and turned her into hummus. I know they have."

"It's just the newness of the store, dear," she reassured me. "In a couple weeks you'll be sauntering down the Beef Brisket Byway like an old timer."

She led me to the front of the store where she had parked our shopping cart, which was now filled with groceries from the highways and byways of Fred and Bubba's.

"Now you stay here with the cart while I go over to that trendy little bank over there and take out a loan for the groceries," she said.

Well, at least some things about Fred and Bubba's haven't changed.

"Like a lot of mothers, mom was never satisfied that there was enough to eat for Thanksgiving dinner. She would always prepare enough food for sixteen people just in case someone suddenly dropped in unexpectedly for dinner on Thanksgiving."

STALKING THANKSGIVING

Thanksgiving always reminds me of family, food and indigestion.

Every year for Thanksgiving my mom would always make for my dad and I and my brother a 15 pound turkey filled with three pounds of stuffing. She'd also make a kettle of mashed potatoes, a bucket of gravy, plus two green salads, one with endive which I hated but everyone else loved.

Mom was also big on vegetables. For Thanksgiving we'd always have at least seven vegetables on the table. The veggie selection usually included my father's favorite candied sweet potatoes, then whole corn, cream corn, French cut green beans with mushrooms, sweet peas, carrots, broccoli and Brussels sprouts. If we didn't eat another lick of vegetables all year, we got our fill on Thanksgiving.

To make sure no one walked away from the table hungry, my mother would also put out black olives, green olives, several different kinds of cheeses, relish, pickles, hot peppers, plus a couple loaves of bread and biscuits. Sometimes, if she had enough time, mom would make soup to start.

There were always three pies sitting in the wings for desert. We'd have apple, pumpkin and cherry pies that had to be consumed with whipped cream. Every other Thanksgiving she would also throw together a small cake for good measure in case anyone still was hungry. In preparation for this meal you had to start fasting three days before hand.

Mom worried about drop ins

Like a lot of mothers, mom was never satisfied that there was enough to eat for Thanksgiving dinner. She would always prepare enough food for sixteen people just in case someone suddenly dropped in unexpectedly for dinner on Thanksgiving.

It would take her six days to prepare the dinner, which we usually gobbled up during the 20 minute half-time of the Lions and Bears game.

One of my fondest memories of those Thanksgivings was the celery stalks. As a special treat every year, mom would take celery stalks, cut them into three foot-lengths and fill them with cream cheese. She would put them on the table before dinner was ready and then scold everyone for eating them. She would then hide them away in the refrigerator until mid-way through dinner, when mom would remember the celery, bring it out, and put one on top everyone's plate of food.

For some reason in our house you could only eat celery stalks with cream cheese on Thanksgiving and sometimes Christmas. One time I got a taste for it in the middle of July and my mother caught me eating celery and cream cheese. She took it away from me saying "Don't eat that now, you'll spoil your Thanksgiving dinner."

Another favorite recipe of my mother's for Thanksgiving was orange jello and chopped pineapple with chunks of cream cheeses floating in it.

The pineapple, cream cheese, orange jello was always the last thing to be served for Thanksgiving dinner. It was always the last thing because my mother would forget to put it out until we had eaten all of the turkey, mashed potatoes, gravy, seven different vegetables, stuffing, salads, and three kinds of pie with whipped cream.

Every year she would find it tucked away in the back of the refrigerator and make us come back to the table and eat it.

Getting together with relatives

I remember one year my mother decided it would be nice to get together with her sister, my Aunt Bertha, and her family for Thanksgiving dinner. Why they did this, I have no idea, unless it was to expand all our bellies until they exploded since both women traditionally cooked huge amounts of food for the annual feast.

The only difference between the two meals was that my Uncle Eddie didn't like turkey, and would only eat roast beef on holidays and Sundays. So at least we were saved from having to eat two turkeys.

Instead we had a 15 pound turkey, a seven pound roast, two kettles of mashed potatoes, 14 vegetables and double the quantities of pickles, olives, cheeses and breads we usually had.

It was a 20-course meal for eight people with leftovers to spare for a small middle east country.

I still don't know why we got together with them that Thanksgiving. My mother and her sister never got along in the kitchen. While the two could co-exist in every other room in the house, the kitchen was a culinary battleground for the two.

That year they got into a fight over how to shred lettuce for salads. The fight started at noon and extended through dinner and into the early evening. One tore lettuce across the grain, while the other tore in lengthwise. Neither one could see the other's point of view.

We had four green salads for dinner that year and all of us were put on the spot to vote on which was the better made salad. But we wouldn't commit, claiming all the salads were great. Except Uncle Eddie, who was a no-nonsense ex-Marine and quick thinker. He dumped his four salads into one bowl and said it all tasted like lettuce to him.

Unfortunately, those days are gone now. My brother lives in California, I'm in Michigan, the cousins have gone to God. My dad who loved sweet potatoes at Thanksgiving died two years ago and Uncle Eddie, the stalwart Marine who would eat nothing but roast beef on Thanksgiving, passed away last year.

Mom and Aunt Bertha are still around and still arguing over how to make the perfect salad. But the real fight's gone out of them; it's only the memory of that dinner they argue about now.

Still, my family helps keep those traditions alive. My wife, Madeline, through some inherited gene given to all moms, still makes for Thanksgiving a 15 pound turkey, the kettle of mashed potatoes, three pounds of stuffing, a bucket of gravy, seven vegetables, two green salads, olives, cheeses, pickles and relish, two breads, dinner rolls and three pies.

And she puts out the three foot celery stalks with cream cheese before dinner and then scolds everyone for eating them. And in honor of my mom, Madeline makes the orange jello with pineapple and chunks of cream cheese floating in it. She even hides it in the refrigerator until everybody's eaten dinner and then makes us come back to the table to eat it.

Chapter IV

THE BASEBALL DIARIES

I once lost my mind and became the coach of my son's baseball team. They were the worst team in the history of baseball and I knew nothing about coaching. But together we pulled off the impossible.

"The best way to watch any children's sport is to sit in the stands, applauding the good plays and groaning at the bad breaks through the duct tape you've pasted over your mouth."

THE BASEBALL DIARIES - YEAR 1: HOW I BECAME A COACH

Rummaging through my closet the other day, I came across an old baseball that had been carefully wrapped in plastic, stored away and totally forgotten, as we tend to do with our most precious mementos.

As I unwrapped the ball, the smell of fresh-cut grass, chalk lines, and the lingering aroma of 14 pre-teens who had just celebrated the end of a winning season over pepperoni pizza, filled the room.

I looked at the names of the players signed in childish scrawls over the leather ball. In an open space along the seams, someone had inked in "To Coach. 24 - 0."

For those of you who know little about baseball, a 24 and 0 record is a perfect season. A flawless 24 games when my dream team out hit, out ran and out scored every other team in our league.

It was the highlight of my career coaching seven-to nine-year-olds in the fine art of baseball. I later went on to coach much more normal, losing teams, but this was one of those once in a lifetime seasons when all the stars and planets fell into line and a bunch of boys and their coaches pulled it all together for one glorious summer.

It didn't start out that way, though. In fact, I never intended to coach a kid's baseball team. I came to coaching baseball like most overweight, out-of-shape jocks, who think they're still 16 and wind up heading Little League, Tyke and T-ball teams. I became a coach because I opened my big mouth and started telling my son's baseball coach what was wrong with his team.

I later learned, too late, that the best way to watch any children's sport is to sit in the stands, applauding the good plays and groaning at the bad breaks through the duct tape you've pasted over your mouth. You save yourself a lot of trouble that way and coaches appreciate it more than you can ever imagine.

The making of a coach

Anyway, my son's coach took my unerring advice from the stands through several practices, grunting at what I said with the scowl of a battle-weary veteran. Then he ignored it. At the end of my son's third practice, though, he called me over to his car.

"You know I'm too old for this," he said, wiping a film of dirt and baseball sweat from his face. "What this team needs is a younger coach with new ideas," he said, handing me a bag of bats and balls. "I think you're that man."

And before I could even provide a modest protest, he hopped in his car and sped away. I rushed home that night and announced the good news to my wife.

"Guess who's just been named the new coach of our son's team," I announced proudly.

"Hopefully, someone who is not standing in this room?" she responded supportively.

But I would not be deterred from the joy of the moment. "Just think of it, I'm the coach of Nathan's team. This is going to be a monumental summer," I said.

While I was imagining taking this team to the World Series, my wife burst my bubble.

"Do you know anything about coaching?" she asked.

That's the problem with people who aren't sports oriented — they focus on the minor details rather than seeing the big picture.

"I know enough," I said defensively, figuring I could draw on my experience as a Little Leaguer 25 years ago. Plus, as a sporadic, life-long follower of the Chicago Cubs, I figured I could wing it.

Who's on First?

I'll never forget my first night of coaching. As I walked onto the field, 14 boys in a variety of shapes, sizes and colors surrounded me, shouting 100 different questions all at the same time.

"Can I play first base? Can I play second base? Can I pitch? When am I batting? What time's practice over? Can my dog stay in the dogout? When do we get our uniforms? Where's the bathrooms? Can we go home now?"

Setting the equipment bag down, I quieted them as best I could and began the carefully prepared speech that I had worked on all day. A speech that was designed to inspire them with a sense of destiny and excitement at the journey they were about to embark upon by participation in the game of baseball.

I got about five words into my talk when the team discovered the equipment bag. Within a matter of seconds there were 14 little kids standing in a tight-knit circle around me, trying to kill each other with baseball bats.

"Drop the bats," I yelled, pulling bats out of the hand of two youngsters who were gleefully ignoring me while they whacked at each other with Louisville Sluggers. "Everybody sit."

That's when I made the first of several hundred impromptu "coach's rules" that would see us safely through the season with no major head wounds.

"No one touches a bat unless told to, and no one swings a bat unless they're in the batter's box or on-deck circle," I said, explaining the significance of those two safety areas that had been created by the Baseball Commission to protect little kids and their coaches.

Then, I spent the next 10 minutes answering questions provoked by the new rules. "Can I touch the bat if Jimmy tells me to? What if my mom tells me to touch a bat? What if the bat accidentally touches me?" I ended all discussion on bat touching by sending them onto the field for some fielding practice.

Now, in fielding practice, it is generally accepted that there is one player for each position. At the age level I was coaching, I discovered most players prefer to work in small groups of five to six, standing on top of one another, like they're waiting for a bus. When a ball is hit in their direction, they all charge in a pack, pushing and shoving until one leaps on the moving sphere and the rest pile on top.

In the brief span of a few minutes of fielding, I created seven more rules and discovered that coaching my kid's baseball team was not going to be as easy as I thought.

In fact, as my players tripped over bases, jumped high into the air to catch grounders, and picked dandelions in the outfield, I suddenly realized that I knew nothing about coaching baseball, and worse yet, my players knew even less about the game than I did.

A long season in the making

Even though I played baseball as a youth, I was terrible at the game. I was always the last to be picked, always the last to bat. I played the required, bare-minimum two innings in the field, during which I and my coach prayed no one would hit the ball to me. And here I was, taking on an inexperienced, hard-luck ball team that showed no promise, whose chances for a winning season were slim and none.

It was going to be one very long season, I thought as I headed home that night, my son at my side. I began doubting the wisdom of having taken on coaching responsibilities. "Why am I doing this?" I wondered, just as my son interrupted my doubts.

"How'd I do tonight?" he asked.

"You did great, son. You did just fine," I answered, knowing in that instant why I had become a coach.

"So when can I play second base?" he asked.

We were the "Owls," the worst team in the history of organized baseball. A team so bad that parents were known to move to different towns if their kid was picked for the Owls. But we were destined for greatness.

THE BASEBALL DIARIES YEAR 2: THE BAD NEWS OWLS

The first season I ever coached organized kids baseball I went out and rented the movie "The Bad News Bears." It's a movie about how this inspired coach takes over a Little League baseball team of misfits and losers and they go from the bottom of the league to contenders for the championship in one season. That's exactly how I envisioned my first season of coaching.

Unfortunately, things don't always work out like they do in the movies. The only thing my team and the movie had in common was that we were last place in the league.

We were the "Owls," the worst team in the history of organized baseball. A team with a tradition of bad teams spanning decades. I looked in the record books and talked to old timers, and found this team had never won a league championship, and only had one winning season in nearly 20 years of play. The team was so bad that parents were known to sell their homes and move to different towns if their kid was picked for the Owls.

But the Owls were my team, and they were all future all-stars in my eyes, especially if I squinted real hard when they were on the field.

I have already confessed that I knew nothing about coaching. It was only through a combination of pluck and stupidity that I became coach of this team. Which kind of worked well, because even though I knew nothing about coaching, the players on my team knew even less about playing baseball, so we all started out about even.

Trapping the wily assistant coach

The people that actually knew everything about coaching baseball were the parents sitting in the stands. They could tell me everything I was doing wrong and advise me on who should be played where and when with an unerring sense of baseball that would have made the great New York Yankee's manager Casey Stengel proud.

Towards the end of our first day of practice, one of the fathers sitting in the bleachers decided he could take no more, and came down to the edge of the field with some advice.

"I think that kid out in center field might make a good infielder," he confided, pointing to a tall, hyperactive player named Ritchie, who was at that moment running in circles pulling up dandelions and throwing them in the air. "He almost caught the ball the last time you hit it at him," the father said.

I looked at the kid and somehow knew that Ritchie was this guy's son. Then I looked at the the man and it was like looking in a mirror. Here was another father, like myself, who desperately wanted his kid to be a great ball player on a great team, but was hampered by an idiot coach.

I looked at him and saw this raw need to be part of this team written all over his face. If I had been a real coach, I would have thanked him for his advice and gone off and ignored him like every other good coach would have done. But I wasn't a real coach, so I said: "Hey, you've got a real good eye. Why don't give me a hand with the infield players."

You would have thought I offered him a presidential cabinet post. "You mean it? You want me to help out?" he asked, and without waiting for a reply, he jumped over the fence and and began organizing the infield players. I had hooked my first assistant coach. By the end of the week, I had snagged five more assistant coaches using the same technique.

I may not have had the best team in the league, but I was going to have the largest coaching staff ever assembled in the history of kids' baseball. I had infield coaches, outfield coaches, batting and throwing coaches, base coaches. One guy did nothing but keep track of the score book during the game and another took the balls and bats home every night and washed them.

The bully

With the coaching duties under control, I could concentrate on turning this team into a finely oiled, winning machine. And the first thing I did was get rid of the best player on our team. He was our catcher, a big hulking kid, who when he wasn't spitting tobacco juice on home plate and hitting home runs, spent his spare time terrorizing his teammates by getting them in a strangle hold and trying to pop their little heads off.

I think we probably could have worked out the head-popping thing, but he also had this annoying habit of taking himself out of games at will, and changing positions when the spirit moved him. That didn't sit well with me as a coach, and finally a couple games into the season I gave him an ultimatum: "Either play where I put you or sit in the dugout." He answered me by picking up a bag of bats that was still attached to the bat boy and flinging it across the field. "I quit," he said, stalking out of the field.

"That went pretty well," I thought. But then the hard part came. I had to tell the team and the assistant coaches that I had forced the best player on our team, if not the entire league, to quit. I expected tears and lamentation when I made the announcement, but instead everybody cheered. That's when I learned that nobody likes a bully, even if they can hit .400 in the regular season.

Hard as it is to believe, we became a better team after that. Oh sure, players still slid into first base, and a few of the infielders sometimes would wander away from their bases in search of butterflies, but the essence that makes a team started to come together.

We needed a catcher and got Jerome

I learned to use the strengths and weaknesses of the players to our advantage. I put Ritchie, who was a perpetual motion machine, on third base to distract the other teams' batters. We found one of our kids was a basketball player who could snag overthrown balls right out of the air. I made him a first baseman. My son Nathan, who was still getting the hang of catching a baseball, proved to be a terror in the batter's box.

What we were lacking was a good catcher. We needed someone with the speed and agility of a lynx in that position. Someone who — bound by face mask, chest protector, knee and shin guards — could catch the ball, jump up from a kneeling position and throw the ball halfway across the field to put out a runner trying to steal second base. That's what we needed. Instead we got Jerome.

Jerome was one of those players who did everything right, but did it in slow motion. Jerome could catch and had an arm that could rifle the ball to any spot he aimed at. It just took a while. In the first game he played, everyone who got to first, stole second base effortlessly. By the third inning, the opposing team's runners were stealing two bases at a time and laughing at poor Jerome. We lost that game by the 10-run mercy rule in the fourth inning.

Word spread through the league that our catcher was slow as molasses and was an easy two-base steal for any runner. I wasn't buying it, though. Jerome was slow, but he had a good arm, so I told him to just forget second base. Let them steal it, but if anybody dared trespass towards third he had orders to take them down. It took our next opponents, the Colts, six consecutive tag outs at third base before they realized Jerome wasn't going to let them get there. We won that game by two runs and no one ever laughed at Jerome again.

We went on to win six more games that season and finished 7 and 9. It wasn't a winning season, but it was one of the best records the Owls had ever had. The parents couldn't have been happier. The kids were ecstatic. The coaches were overjoyed. We were destined for greatness. I could feel it. "Just wait 'til next year," I predicted, finally starting to act like a real coach.

*The name "Owls" just didn't strike fear in the hearts of
the other ball teams. I figured that unless we started
playing baseball teams called the "Field Mice"
and "Squirrels," we needed a better name.*

THE BASEBALL DIARIES-YEAR 3:
THE PERFECT SEASON

The hardest part about being a coach for your kid's baseball team
is learning all the players' names. Eight-and nine-year-olds all look
alike to me.

I'm sure that's why God created baseball uniforms. Up until my
teams got their uniforms each year, I'd just go around calling all my
players "Tiger" or "Slugger." It sounded better than "hey you" and it
seemed to build their confidence.

Once they got uniforms with numbers on their back, though, I could
boldly call out "nice catch number seven" and "good hit, five."

The year my rag-tag team the "Owls" got it all together with a 24 -
0 season, I had a surprise for them on uniform day. We were getting rid
of our stupid yellow and white uniforms that made us look like spoiled
cream puffs in favor of blue and white duds that made us look like
ballplayers. I also had another surprise for them.

We had finished our first season 7 and 9, and went on to an incred-
ible 11 and 7 finish our second year. But deep down in my coach's
heart, I knew a team called the Owls was only going to go so far in this
world. The name "Owls" just didn't strike fear in the hearts of the other
ball teams. I figured that unless we started playing teams called the
"Field Mice" and "Squirrels," we needed a better name.

So at the start of our third season we became the RAMS!!!! It
might have been my imagination, but the boys seemed to walk taller,
hit better and had more confidence as the Rams. They also stopped that
annoying cheer: "Whooo, Whoooo, Whooooo we going to beat" and
instead just butted heads.

Luck of the draft

That spring we totally lucked out in the baseball tryouts where
new players are picked. We got Ernie on our first pick. Ernie was one
of those ballplayers coaches love because they do everything you tell

them. You say, "Ernie, go to second base" and he does it. You tell Ernie to steal home and he does it. You say "Ernie, I'd like you to hit an infield, home run off the right-field fence and run the bases backwards" and Ernie will do it.

Along with Ernie I managed somehow to pick up "the Glove," the best 8-year-old short stop who ever lived. But along with "the Glove" I also got his dad, "Big Glove," who would sit in the stands during the games preparing written critiques on the team, its coaching and the general state of baseball.

One of the things he really didn't like about our team was that everybody got a chance to bat first during the season, no matter how good or bad they were at hitting the ball.

Every other coach in the world puts their best hitters up first and then the lesser batters. But, I figured everybody worked hard and deserved a spot in the limelight. It was worth a few bad starts to watch those kids count the games until they were lead-off batter and see the pride they had as they walked to the plate.

A strange thing happened, though. Kids who couldn't hit a ball to save their life batting eighth, started slugging the ball when they batted first. We were unstoppable. We went through the first nine games of the season without a problem. The 10th game, I and a few of the other coaches had to be out of town so I asked "Big Glove," the baseball expert, to take over the team for the night.

"I'm glad you asked me, I've got a few ideas for the team I've wanted to try out," he said, tapping a leather briefcase bulging with game plans.

Big Glove was waiting on my doorstop when I got home the next night. The Rams, he said, had won by only one run in extra innings. The game ended in a coaches' brawl, in which one coach lost the tip of his finger when a parent bit it off.

"Don't ever leave this team with me again," he said, as he handed over the equipment and ran for his car.

The real thrill of coaching

My greatest thrill as a coach came a couple games before the end of the season. We were 20 and 0 and were playing our arch rivals the Colts, who were in second place. But there were signs this wasn't going to be a good game. Our first baseman was out with an injury, the "Glove" had gone into a slump and the heavens were dark and overcast. We jumped off to a good start but were only one run ahead in the fourth inning when the Colts got up to bat and went on a hitting spree to score six runs.

My team came off the field with tears streaming down their little faces. "We're going to lose," they wailed, throwing their gloves on the ground. They were devastated; their perfect season was coming to an end.

No matter what I said to encourage them, they just looked at me with their tear-stained eyes and wailed: "We're going to lose." In our turn at bat we managed to get back a couple runs, but watching those kids prepare to go back on the field, I knew we wouldn't win unless I did something to snap them out of it.

So I did. I benched the whole team. "The only players going out on the field are those who think we're going to win. We'll play with half a team if we have to," I said.

Ernie was the first off the bench and on to the field. "Coach says we got to win the game," he chanted as the rest of the kids followed him out.

Although we played tough, the Colts were tougher. The first three batters all got on base and we were facing their biggest slugger with the bases loaded and no outs.

One big hit would clear the bases, destroying whatever confidence was left in my demoralized team. Silently I prayed for a strikeout I knew would never happen.

The Colts' big slugger connected hard on the very first pitch, slashing a high line drive over our shortstop. The ball was sailing straight towards the left field fence when a glove shot up in the air and stopped it cold.

My son Nathan had saved three runs. And while we cheered wildly, Nathan took the ball out of his glove, and did what we had trained the outfielders to do for three long seasons. He threw the ball to second base, caught the runner off the bag, and got a double play.

That was the spark we needed. We won the game by one run, and never looked back.

I see some of my players from the Rams once in a while. They're young men in their 20s now, some with little ballplayers of their own. Whenever we talk, I still call them "Tiger" and "Slugger." And they still call me "Coach."

Chapter V

PUMPING LAUNDRY

I'm a spectator when it comes to sports and exercise. Even though I can't bench press my weight in laundry, I know how to get a cushy seat on my mountain bike, fix the problems with golf and achieve illusional health.

The trend of using exercise equipment to hang clothes and laundry in our house developed out of a sense of guilt that these healthful machines were sitting around not getting any use.

RECYCLE THAT EXERCISE BIKE

I'm proud to say my family owns every piece of exercise equipment ever invented.

I don't know why I'm proud to say this, except that it gives the impression we might actually use this stuff.

The truth is we do use exercise equipment, but not for the purpose it was intended. For example, the Nordic Ski simulator in our bedroom makes an excellent clothes rack. You can hang two to three weeks' worth of clothes on the contraption before it ever looks overwhelmed.

We also keep an exercise bike in our laundry room that is ideal for hanging freshly washed shirts and pants right from the dryer on the handle bars. The bike seat also makes a convenient place to rest when you're folding towels. And the pedals are a great holding site for lost socks.

I think the trend of using exercise equipment to hang clothes and laundry in our house developed out of a sense of guilt that these healthful machines were sitting around not getting any use. At least with clothes hanging on them, they seemed to be serving a purpose.

Bench press your clothes

In fact, exercise equipment has become an essential part of our household. When we built our house a few years ago, my wife and I debated whether to put an extra closet in the master bedroom, or just buy more exercise equipment. The equipment won out because it not only can be used to store clothes, but you can do other things with it, like exercise. A closet, on the other hand, has limited exercise potential.

To give you an idea of how good this stuff is for wardrobe care, we have one of those large, Nautilus weight training systems in our living room. Each family member has their own section and all of us use it for free-style clothes hanging. This piece of equipment also doubles as furniture. It has several nice, comfy benches we use to stretch out on while watching television. And when we have company, we can pull it up to the dining room table as extra chairs for guests.

Just so you don't think these machines aren't getting an honest workout once in a while, my one son is currently building up his upper torso by doing weight training on the Nautilus. I'm proud to say he can now bench press 220 pounds, four pairs of dress slacks and a half-dozen shirts. I think we have the makings of a new Olympic sport here.

Not all pieces of exercise equipment are immediately recognizable for their haberdashery potential. For example, it took us a long time to figure out what to do with a rowing machine we bought because it has very little storage space on its single 12-inch seat. You can only stack about a half day's worth of clothes there before they tumble over.

But, when we took it into the kids' bathroom, stood it on end and extended the rowing arms, we found it became a convenient drying rack for wet towels.

Don't be a dumbbell

Exercise equipment also has other uses besides hanging and drying clothes. Take the big punching bag, sometimes called the "heavy bag," which can be laid on its side in the family room for use as a foot rest. It's also much cheaper than buying a conventional Ottoman.

The small hand dumbbells that are used for building up wrist power and upper arm strength are great for propping open doors.

The stairmaster is terrific for stacking books and magazines on the two conveniently located steps. We just put the magazines on one stair and the books on the other and then when we want something, all we do is flip a switch and the machine brings the desired pile up to us without our having to bend over too far.

Jump ropes can be stretched tight between basement rafters for the storage of winter coats, or in a pinch they are a handy dog leash when the real thing isn't available.

Even those hand grip things you use to build up hand strength, when set inside of a favorite tie, will hold its crisp shape for months. I'm thinking of sending that one to Heloise.

Running shoes can be bronzed and used for book ends. And those new "Abercisers" that help tighten up those abdominal muscles, are really nifty too. Just stuff them with pillows and they make great backrests.

Even the boxes the exercise equipment came in can serve a purpose. We store all our exercise manuals, aerobic tapes and workout clothes in them.

One of the most unique uses for exercise equipment we can claim was my own invention. Sick and tired of having the kids throw dirty clothes all over their room, I put an electronic treadmill up on a table in the room where they now stack all of their dirty clothes. Once a week we bring down the laundry baskets, turn on the treadmill and it dumps the dirty clothes right into the baskets.

Actually the only piece of exercise equipment we never found an alternate use for was the "Thighmaster." It just sat around the house for a long time, thighless, until finally, overcome by the pressure of having a useless piece of exercise equipment around the house, we threw it out.

"My family suggested I needed a bike for exercise. But I protested "I've got a bike," referring to the pile of rusting metal at the edge of the driveway where I parked it five years before. **❧**

BIKING IT

The other day my family decided I was getting a little overweight and I needed to get off my "pleasingly plump" buttocks and do something physical.

"I'm too busy working to exercise," I said, wiping Cheetos crumbs from my hands before finishing my 40th game of Space Invaders on the computer.

They suggested I needed to buy a bike.

"I've got a bike," I protested, referring to the pile of rusting metal at the edge of the driveway where I parked it five years before.

"And it's practically new. It's hardly ever been ridden," I said.

"Besides, I get plenty of exercise, I walk at least a mile a day," I said in my own defense.

"Going to the refrigerator 84 times a day doesn't count as exercise," my wife Madeline said.

I started to tell her that someone had to make sure the refrigerator light was still working, but she wasn't buying any of it. "You need exercise," she insisted.

"But it's almost winter, and I downhill ski," I whined.

"Falling down a lot isn't exercise," insisted my youngest son, who's seen me ski.

I reminded them that I have this history of fighting "chronic fatigue syndrome" which requires me to lay around on the sofa a lot.

"Tough it out," my ungrateful brood chimed.

"Listen," my wife said. "Either you go down and buy a bike or I'll buy one for you. And I hope you like your bike pink with flowers on the pedals."

I knew she would do it too, because I still have the lavender suit she bought me when I wouldn't refresh my aging wardrobe. I still wear it once a year for her on Mother's Day.

Just another Geek in Spandex

Besides, deep in my heart — which sets somewhere just above my middle-aged paunch — I knew they were right. So the next day, after a hearty breakfast, I went off in search of a fine, new cycling machine that would, with use, return me to the fighting weight of a novice Sumo wrestler.

Now the last time I bought a bike, brakes were still an optional accessory, so I decided to stop and get some advice on bike selection from some experts. I found out right away that buying a new bike is not the simple "give me the red one over there" experience it used to be. For one thing, you don't go to the local general merchandising retailer anymore for bikes. So declared my cycling advisors, two 10-year-olds I met on the street.

"You got to go to a cycle store, or you'll be just another geek on a (brand name bike I hesitate to mention here for fear of a lawsuit)," they said. Not wanting to be just another geek, I took their advice and went to the local cycling emporium "Mike's Bikes." I sauntered in and was greeted by a sinewy young lady, decked out in Lycra Spandex riding shorts, with an entry number from the "Tour de France" still pinned to her shirt.

Where's the busted tricycle?

"Do you have mountain bikes?" I asked, tossing out a name I had heard my cycling consultants mention.

"We just got in a new Trek, super-light, carbon-fiber frame, all terrain, all-weather, dual-suspension, adjustable-shock, 24-gear model I think you'd enjoy," she offered, showing me a bike that looked like you could move furniture with it.

"How much is it?" I asked, getting right to the heart of the deci-sion-making process.

"Only $4,000 and change," she said blithely, with what I thought was a remarkably straight face.

"What can I get for the change part?" I asked.

"We've got a busted tricycle in the basement," she replied, look-ing around the store for a real customer she might be able to help.

"What do you want to spend?" she finally asked, not spotting anyone.

I mentioned an amount and, when she stopped laughing, she showed me a nice mountain bike I could get started with for a mere $700.

Although it was drastically more than I wanted to spend, I realized if I didn't buy something, my wife would, and it would cost more and have Easter Bunnies painted on it.

"I'll take it," I said, figuring the cost was cheaper than a liposuction operation anyway.

"We'll need to get you measured," she said, explaining that proper arm and leg fit were essential to comfortable biking.

"Just make sure it has a good kick stand," I said, while having my arms and legs measured in different awkward biking positions. "And I'll need a padded, cushy seat on it," I added.

She looked at me like I had just asked her to kill a puppy.

"We don't put cushy seats on mountain bikes," she said with disdain. "You'll look like a geek."

"But a comfortable geek," I thought. The truth is I had one of those concrete hard, bun-bruising racing seats on my last bike, which is why it sat in my driveway so much.

"It's cushy seat or no sale," I declared, imagining how good a wide, soft, padded, leather seat would feel on my ample behind. But I needed a good reason to have it.

Hard seats don't cover the spread

"The truth is ma'am, I have a physical problem that won't let me use uncomfortable bike seats," I said, picturing a rear view shot of me pedaling up the street with most of my behind hanging off the bike seat.

After consulting with the World Cycling Council, or something, she permitted me to purchase a padded, cushy seat with my mountain bike if I promised to later bring in a doctor's excuse for my disability.

As we wrapped up the bank loan for my new bike, cushy seat, Spandex cycling shorts, and a hideous biking helmet that looked like the head of one of those monsters from "Alien," she handed me some pamphlets on mountain biking in Colorado.

"You'll probably want to take a trip out west to the Rockies to get full enjoyment of your new mountain bike," she said.

"You mean I spent a small fortune on a bike and I've got to go to Colorado to enjoy it," I stuttered, shocked at the undisclosed catch.

"I thought 'mountain bike' was a cute name, like 'English Racer' or 'Lighting Streak,' I mumbled, while she explained the pure pleasure of spending all day pedaling up an 8,000-foot mountain trail and then risking your life and limb to get back down.

"I'll take it under advisement," I said walking my new bike to the car, knowing full well it would never see any elevation higher than my garage wall. I've got to admit, though, I really do enjoy my new mountain bike. I ride it almost every day to the ice cream store down the street and there's this little hill on the way I can now ride over with ease.

"Golf has traditionally been a gentlemen's sport, except when played by me, my cohorts and of course the Ladies Professional Golf Association."

LET'S MAKE GOLF A BLOOD SPORT

I don't usually make comment on the world of sports, but something so unusual happened last week that it deserves exploration.

I'm talking about the Ryder Cup golf match in which the best of the American golfers played the best of the European golfers.

Golf, as we all pretty well know, has traditionally been a gentlemen's sport, except when played by me, my cohorts and of course the Ladies Professional Golf Association.

On the whole, golfers are a fairly milktoastie bunch in comparison to athletes who play football or rugby. Last week's Ryder Cup challenge changed all that.

This biannual match in the past was always a friendly, good-will game between two great golfing powers. It's primarily been friendly because the Americans have won it some 500 times and Europeans didn't have much to say. But that's changed in the past few outings, since the Europeans started eating our lunch on the course and at the country club after the matches.

This time before the two 12-man teams met, there was none of the usual pleasantries as in the past. Before this year, you'd hear the players say: "I think they've fielded an outstanding team this year, but we've got better dressed caddies." This year the teams got down in the dirt, bad talking each other just like they were the Chicago Bulls or Green Bay Packers.

The only problem is bad talking sounds threatening when it comes from a 320-pound lineman named Bronco Nagerski, but loses credibility when coming from a guy named "Colin" who looks like he just stepped off a cruise ship.

What's a 1/2 point?

Sports writers had a field day building up this tremendous grudge match between these two dozen guys with creases in their slacks. In the end, after all the hype of how this team was going to tear up that team, the match wound up some ridiculous score like 13 1/2 to 14 1/2 in favor of the Europeans.

What kind of a score is that? What big-time, manly sport awards a half point to someone? That sounds like someone missed a field goal in football but they gave him a 1/2 point for style.

If golf is ever going to have the same mass appeal as other blood and guts televised sports, it's got to get in tune with the times. For one thing, golfers need to do something about their names. Monikers like Tommy Kite and Davis Love III, just don't make it in the tough arena of head-bashing sports.

Golfers need to adopt nicknames that would give meat to their threats. They need names like Colin "The Barbarian" Montgomerie and Mark "The Hangman" O'Meara and Seve "The Clubber" Ballesteros. Then when they say "we're going to beat on these dudes" it might mean something.

Bigger scores to win

In addition to nicknames, something has to be done with the scoring in golf. Really, when you stop to think about it, these guys played 524 holes of golf over four days and came up with what is essentially a mediocre football score.

Golf scoring is backwards because the less you score the more you win. This is just the opposite of most civilized sports. I think we need to change the scoring of the game. Instead of having the low score win, let's make it a blood sport with high scoring.

Face it, watching a 20-hour golf game when the winner comes in "five under" doesn't do much for sports headlines. What they should do is assign 25 points for every par made, 50 points for birdies, 100 points for eagles and 250 points for a "hole in one."

Then you'd generate some real golf excitement when the television announcer goes "the Americans trashed the Europeans 2,350 to 1,200 today in match play." That would be exciting golf.

But scoring is only part of it. Something needs to be done with the whole game to make it more interesting for today's audiences. Basically what you have is a 190-pound white guy hitting a little round ball toward a hole in the ground about the size of a teacup. They need to put some pizzazz in the game from tee to green.

Let's change the rules

Why not time the speed of the golfer's swing on the tee just like they do pitched in baseballs. Although club speed doesn't dictate how well the shot is hit, it would give sports writers a whole new category of irrelevant sports statistics they can quote. Fans would love that kind of stuff.

"Tiger Woods' swing on that drive was 148 mph," says Jim McKay. "To bad he hit a tree or that ball would have been out of here."

Another problem with golf is it's incredibly hard for the average fan to watch that little white ball float up to the sky and then land like a speck 300 yards down the fairway. What they need to do, to get some visual excitement in the game, is create a golf ball that gives off sparks and trails smoke as it flies through the air. It also wouldn't hurt if the ball exploded on impact. You know, to perk up the game.

Get fans involved

There's also great potential to create more excitement if golfers make better use of their equipment. Except for sports that use guns and live ammunition, there is probably no more lethal equipment than the stuff found in the average golf bag. They carry 14 long clubs in there with chunks of metal welded on the end. Think of the potential here — full body contact golf.

What also makes golf boring to watch is that players who aren't hitting, stand around with nothing to do. I'd like to see them go out in the fairway when the other players are hitting and try to catch the ball with a baseball mitt. If they successfully catch a ball, they should be allowed to throw it in the woods or a nearby lake.

I can hear Jim McKay now: "It's a beautiful drive right down the center of the fairway, but wait, Seve Ballesteros has caught it and he's stuffing it down a gopher hole. What a bad break for Davis Love."

Let's face it, what really makes professional sports exciting is the fans. Until the fans get more involved as part of the game, golf is never going to be a real spectators' sport. The day I see half-naked fans in day-glo paint chanting "dunk that putt," is the day golf makes it into the hearts of America.

*"Curly's a big Green Bay Packer fan who paints himself green
and gold for every game and wears a cheese hat on his head.
About midway through this season we discovered the
hat was made of real cheese."*

SUPER BOWL SALAD

The Super Bowl experience, experts agree, is kind of a "guy thing."
The experts, of course, being me and my buddies, who get together
once a year to drink soda, eat chips and watch the most lopsided football game of the year.

The majority of women I know take very little interest in the game.
I offer up as proof my own sweet wife, Madeline, who every February
or March asks me when the Super Bowl is being played.

This year, though, she fooled me. A week before the game she
asked me, "Is the Super Bowl coming up?"

It was a question that raised my defenses and caused the hair to
stand up on the back of my neck.

"Yes. Why?"

"Are you going to watch it?" she asked.

"Are you kidding? This is the biggest game of the year. The decid-
ing 60 minutes of football history that will determine the 'Supreme
Champion' of the season. It's 'Must See TV,' " I explained.

"Well, if this one game decides everything, why do you bother to
watch the other 244 games from July through December?" she asked.

"So I know how the two teams got to the big game," I explained

"Can't you just look that up in old newspapers?" she asked.

"Women obviously know nothing about the tradition of football,"
I responded.

"Explain it to me?" she requested, knowing full well I have a problem explaining things I like to do, such as playing golf or reading magazines backwards. All of which make no sense when you try to explain
them. But I tried anyway.

Explaining football

"Well, you watch the regular season football games, hoping your
team can make it to the playoffs. And then about mid-season you pick
a couple other teams to root for, because it looks like your team won't
be making it. But then your team makes a comeback, and now you've

got three or four teams you're cheering for. Then towards the end of the season you add a few old favorites that you wouldn't mind seeing in playoffs, but don't think will do well in the Super Bowl.

"That way you have at least one team in the big game, you sort of like, sometimes," I said.

"Well, I think it's just an excuse to drink (soda) with your friends, go off your diet and put your feet up on the coffee table, " she suggested.

"I admit, it's a male bonding thing," I explained, knowing she'd like that.

"Well, I'd like to share the Super Bowl with you this year, and do some bonding of our own," my wife suggested.

I almost choked on my soda.

"You wouldn't like it," I said.

"Why?" she asked.

"Because it doesn't involve.... there's too much... and that other stuff... you see," I blithely explained.

"It doesn't have to be just us. We could invite your friends and their wives and make a party out of it," she suggested. "A Super Bowl Party."

Like that'll happen

I could just picture the type of party she had in mind with finger sandwiches on matching Super Bowl plates, a punch bowl with glasses, and probably something healthy, involving fruits and vegetables.

Then I pictured the guys I watch football with. Like there's this guy Larry who drinks his soda (wink, wink) out of a straw attached to cans in a holder on his head.

Then there's Curly, a big Green Bay Packer fan who paints himself green and gold for every game and wears a cheese hat on his head. About midway through this season we discovered the hat was made of real cheese.

"Say, aren't these hats supposed to be made out of foam rubber or something," I asked.

"They were sold out. So I made my own," explained Curly, offering all of us a sample of his hat.

Now I can't imagine Madeline, who has a problem eating veggie dip that has sat out for a few hours, nibbling a sample of Curly's hat, which was probably purchased sometime in August and not refrigerated since.

"We could have some Super Bowl sandwiches," suggested Madeline. "I found a Martha Stewart recipe where you core out a whole water melon and make a stadium out of it using fruits and vegetables to represent the fans in their team colors. The field is made out of spinach dip with carrot sticks for the goal posts."

"To tell you the truth dear, our traditional snacks during the Super Bowl game usually come in a can with resealable lids, so we can save the leftovers for next season," I said.

We tried fancy foods for the big game once. Moe, who watches cooking shows when there's no sports on, decided to make these appetizers out of mushroom caps and sausage that were supposed to look like footballs. They turned out looking like gravel and we didn't eat very many. But we saved them and they were much better the next year.

"We have simple tastes, dear, and a system," I explained. "I bring the pretzels, Curly brings the bean dip, and Larry brings the cheese hat."

"Cheese hat?" she inquired, looking puzzled.

"Never mind," I said.

"So what do you think. Can we have a party?" she asked.

"I guess so," I said, weakening.

"So when's the Super Bowl?" she asked. "It's usually in February or March, isn't it?"

"Yeah, yeah it's March 15. That's the ticket," I said.

Well, I might have to explain that one in a couple months. Or I could just tape the game and replay it. The wives probably wouldn't know the difference, and I know my buddies wouldn't.

"When did we reach the point where muscles on men, and women, are more important than brains, or hair? Both of which I've managed to keep so far."

TEN STEPS TO ILLUSIONAL HEALTH

What's all this obsession these days with fitness and diet? I've got to believe it can't be healthy for you. I'm not talking about the fitness and diet part—those can be beneficial at times in moderation—it's the obsession part that bothers me.

I find it hard to believe the "ideal look" that men and women of all ages are expected to maintain these days. It seems like any woman who is meatier than a drumstick is overweight and any guy that can't iron shirts on his stomach is a slob.

Today some men in their 60s look better than I did when I was a teenager. In fact, today some women at 60 look better than I did as a teenager. But that's not the point. The point is it's downright depressing for the average person to try to compete with the Wonder Women and Chippendale hunks of today. Hardly anyone can realistically measure up to these standards and still work a normal 6 a.m. to 10 p.m. workday.

It's especially annoying when you realize that as little as 40 years ago the ideal American male only had to fill out the armholes of a black T-shirt and be proficient with a bowling ball to be admired as a pillar of the community. Sophia Loren at the time had a figure other women envied. Today she'd be doing ads for the "Big and Large Shop."

Keep your shirt on

I was watching the old movie "Spartacus" recently. It's a movie about a Gladiator revolt during the Roman Empire and the Gladiators in the picture—which were hunkiest of men in the late 1950s, men who were supposed to be tearing wild animals apart with their bare hands—would get laughed off the beach today if they showed up with their shirts off. There was hardly a washboard "Ab" among them.

When did we reach the point where muscles on men, and women, are more important than brains, or hair? Both of which I've managed to keep so far.

I blame it all on Jane Fonda and her obsession to look better at 60 than she did in her 20s. If it wasn't for her silly workout tapes, we could all be enjoying the steady deterioration of our anatomy with dignity as we grow older, just as God intended.

But no. Instead we've got to compete with Hollywood types, magazine models and body builders who have nothing better to do with their time than perform 1,000 sit ups everyday. And for what purpose? Just to make you and I feel bad about ourselves.

Well, I'm mad as heck about it and I'm not going to take any more.

I've decide to take action and find ways to make myself look and feel better without actually doing anything strenuous. I've created a ten step program to illusional health, which you also may want to adopt yourself this year.

The 10 steps

Here's 10 ways to look good without working at it.

1. Hang out with people who are more overweight and out of shape than yourself so you can look good when you're out with them.

2. Avoid people who are thinner and in better shape than yourself, because they probably just want to hang out with you so they can look good.

3. Eliminate all "beauty" magazines from the house. Cancel subscriptions to "Vogue," "Cosmopolitan," "Gentleman's Quarterly" and "Flat Stomach" magazine. Subscribe to "Biker's Digest," "American Hereford Breeder" and Chef Paul Prodhomme's cook books, which usually feature people who weigh lots more than you do but still appear in national magazines and books.

4. Don't bathe. People will stand farther away and you'll look thinner to them.

5. Register for diet and exercise programs, but only go to the "beginner" classes where everyone is overweight and out of shape. Use disguises in case you have to reregister in the same place again.

6. Wear fewer clothes, even in winter. Discard underwear entirely as it adds weight and bulk to your physique.

7. Always stand next to large objects. Multi-story buildings and semi tractor trailer rigs can make you look pounds slimmer.

8. Take up sports that make you look thinner. Do activities like "Monster Truck" rally driving and "Sumo Wrestling" where competi-

tors refer to you as "the skinny one." Avoid activities like swimming and biking which make you wear spandex.

9. Buy larger size clothes so you can claim to have lost weight.

10. Rent the movie "The Maltese Falcon" and study how much better you look than rotund actor Sidney Greenstreet in the character of "Gutman." If more weight is gained during the year, rent "Moby Dick" and study how much better you look than the whale.

Chapter VI

THE TELEMARKETING TERMINATOR

Technology is the Black Plague of modern society. It's eaten up my leisure time and turned my TV against me. Even buying a computer is a life-changing experience. No wonder I became a Telemarketing Terminator.

*❝ The object of "TELEMARKETING TERMINATOR"
is to see how long you can keep a salesperson
on the phone without letting them give you
their sales pitch. I hold the world's record
at 13 minutes and 22 seconds. ❞*

THE TELEMARKETING TERMINATOR

Tired of getting obnoxious phone calls from sales people all the time? Now you can turn the tables on them with a fun new phone game I invented called "TELEMARKETING TERMINATOR."

It doesn't stop the telemarketing calls, but it does make them more enjoyable and loads of laughs.

The object of "TELEMARKETING TERMINATOR" is to see how long you can keep a salesperson on the phone without letting them give you their sales pitch. I hold the world's record at 13 minutes and 22 seconds. And I'm pretty sure it's a world's record since I'm the only one who plays the game right now.

To play, all you need is a stop watch, a telephone and plenty of time to waste talking to people you don't know.

Get your stop watch and start

Here's how it works. A salesperson calls you on the phone. You can usually tell it's a solicitor because they say your full name incorrectly and often. So you start your stop watch and go into your role as the terminator. This first game I recommend you try is called "I can't hear you. Talk louder." It goes like this.

Voice: "Hello. Is this Byron Kukalaka?"
Me: "Hello, Hello. I can't hear you."
Voice: "Hello. Is this Mr. Kukalaka?"
Me: "Can you speak up? I can barely hear you."
Voice: (louder) "Can you hear me now?"
Me: "Yes, that's a little better."
Voice: (still talking loudly) Mr. Kukalaka, I'm Barry Smith from...."
Me: "Wait, you're fading again. Can you talk louder?"
Voice: (Much louder): "I'm Barry Smith from..."
Me: "Owww, you don't have to shout."

From that point you can go into a number of variations. You can tell them they're too loud now and then get them down to almost a whisper. Just make the stuff up as you go along. Tell them you've been having this problem with your phone and ask their advice on what new phone system they might recommend. Or say, you've found the problem, you've got wax build-up in your ear and it's starting to come out. Give a description of the wax as it comes out or ask them to hold on while you get a Q-tip.

I've actually gotten telemarketing people to hang up on me. What a thrill that is. It's like getting a hole-in-one in golf, a grand slam in bridge, Free Parking in Monopoly. And it's worth 100 bonus seconds on your score sheet.

Riddle me this salesman

Another favorite terminator role I call "The Riddler." It goes like this. You get a sales call and you identify yourself, but you tell them before they can go on they have to answer a riddle first. Here's how I play it:

Me: "I'm the Riddle Man. Anyone who calls me has to answer a riddle. My friends love it. People I don't even know call me just to hear my riddles. So if you want to talk to me you've got to answer a riddle first."

Then you ask them a simple riddle like:"Who's buried in Grant's Tomb?"

You'd be surprised how many telemarketing people don't get that one. If they give you the right answer, "Grant;" then protest: "You got it right. I can't believe you guessed it right. That's my hardest riddle. No one ever gets it. Did somebody help you?"

From there you can go into variations, like: "All right it's your turn, ask me a riddle now" or make them answer another riddle because you think they cheated. Then ask them something like: "What state's bird has 10 fingers and 10 toes?" The answer of course is Utah. Then you can say: "I know it is because I 'tah' one there." The less sense these things make, the funnier they become.

Another cute one is "21 Questions." It's the same as the Riddler, except you keep asking them questions. Ask them something like: what is the capital of South Dakota? Then tell them they're right no matter what the answer. Then give them a second question. If they protest, tell them you lied and the capital of South Dakota isn't "Rhode Island" like they said so they have to answer another question. Then ask them something like "What's my favorite color?" then agree no matter what they say. Then go "Okay now for the tie breaker question..." I've never gotten anyone to go beyond the third question.

77

The joke's on them

Another one I've had loads of fun with is "Let me tell you a joke." I usually start off by saying I just heard this really funny joke and I've been stuck in the house all day and I'm dying to tell it to someone. Stress the fact that it's a very short joke. Then make up a really long, pointless story with no punch line. Here's an example.

Me: "There were these three guys, Fred, Bob and Lloyd. Oh, by the way, this is a clean joke. I never repeat off-color jokes even if they are funny. Although there was one about the proctologists that I still chuckle at....(chuckle into phone).... but I won't repeat it because it's kind of off-color. Unless you really want to hear.

"So here's a clean joke you can tell all your friends. You see there were these two guys, Fred and Earl. Or was that three guys? Wait, I think it was three guys. Fred, Earl and Lloyd. I got to get them right, or the joke won't be as funny. What were those names again?"

Voice: "Fred, Bob and Lloyd."

Me: "Have you heard this joke before?"

The object is to just keep telling this inane, pointless story and whenever they want to stop you, just keep saying you're almost done.

I got the world record for this one. Not only did I keep them on the phone for 13 minutes and 22 seconds without giving them a chance to sell me anything, I also got them to hang up on me and got my bonus points.

My last words to them before they hung up were: "Wait. I've got a riddle for you."

*" I predict someday we will use all of our available
time thinking about phone services. In fact,
the only thing phones will be used for
in the future will be to sell you
more phone services"*

LEISURE TIME ON HOLD

Last week while I was rummaging around in the closet for my old disco shoes, I came across an archaeological artifact so rare that it probably hadn't seen the light of day since the dawning of the information age.

It was a book titled "Spare time and what to do with it," written in the early 1980s by leisure-time expert Dr. Tonsa Freetime.

In it, he and other experts predicted that our biggest worry in the future would be what to do with all of our spare time. They were predicting four-day work weeks and so much leisure time, we'd have to hire consultants to help us plan things to fill our daily lives.

As I read snatches of his book through my usual day of work, more work and still more work, I wondered whatever happened to this idiot and what he did with my spare time.

To my amazement, he turned out to be living in Chicago these days running a stress clinic. So I called him up on the phone.

"Dr. Freetime, I just reread your book and wanted to know what happened to all those extra hours we were supposed to have by now in our daily lives?"

The answer he gave shocked me.

"The government deregulated long distance phone calling," said Freetime.

"What!" I exclaimed. "You mean because the government messed with Ma Bell we lost all our spare time."

"That's about it," he said. "When they broke up the monopoly for long-distance calling, they created a vacuum into which every former time-share condo salesman in the country rushed in to sell us telephone services."

Freetime explained that before the breakup, there was one phone company, one phone style, and one phone bill in our world.

"You'd spent maybe ten minutes a month thinking about your long distance phone bill. And most of that time was spent trying to decide whether to call Aunt Edna in Petoskey for her birthday or just send her a card."

"And now?" I asked.

"Today we all spend about ten hours a week answering phone calls from salespeople who can save us a nickel a minute on our phone bills if we call all the people we know between 3 and 4 a.m. on the second Tuesday of every month," he said.

"Then there's the 25 hours a month we spend fielding phone calls selling new telephone services, calling cards and other communication merchandise," said Freetime.

"Finally, we lose a dozen hours a month figuring out the phone bills and why we have all those extra charges," he said. "I predict that someday we will use all of our available time thinking about phone services. In fact, the only thing phones will be used for in the future will be to sell you more phone services."

"Is there no way to stop this? Is there no way to regain all that lost time?" I asked.

"Sure there is. Just retire," he advised. "You see, retired people have the phone system figured out. Just call someone who is retired and then call me back," he said, ending our conversation.

So I called up my mother, who is not only retired but has used the same phone company and the same telephone for the past 50 years.

"Mom," I said, "how do you deal with phone solicitors who want you to switch phone companies?"

"Oh, I don't have any problem with that, I just tell them that they're evil," she said.

"That's all you have to do," I said, surprised.

"Well, they have a comeback if you say you like your present phone company... and they have 20 reasons to switch if you say you don't want to switch," she explained.

"But nobody knows what to say when you tell them they're evil," she said. "Besides, secretly I think they all agree with me."

I admitted she had a point, but I wanted to know how she could resist buying the new telephone technologies like "Caller ID."

"That's easy. I have my own version of Caller ID," she said. "You see, when the phone rings I pick it up and say 'Hello, who is this?' And they tell me. And it doesn't cost me a dime extra."

What about "Call Waiting?" I wanted to know.

"Got that too," she said proudly. "If someone calls me and I'm on the phone, they get a busy signal. So then they have to wait and call me back."

Finally, I asked how much time she spent thinking about her long distance service.

"Oh, about ten minutes a month — and most of that is wondering whether to call Aunt Edna in Petoskey on her birthday, or just send her a card," she said.

Dr. Freetime was right and I called him back to tell him, but he couldn't talk.

"I can't take your call now. I have too many people who are in need of help," he said. "Everyone these days seems all stressed out over whether they are taking full advantage of their ability to call Alaska and Canada for ten cents a minute."

> *I had never thought to look in the mail for money, but sitting in a huge pile of junk mail next to the dog's water bowl was a treasure trove of money I had been ignoring for months.*

COLLIES MAKE LOUSY ACCOUNTANTS

We were a little short of cash the other day and as I was scrounging around the house looking for spare change to pay the mortgage, I discovered a hidden source of cash reserves I never knew we had.

It was the daily mail.

I had never thought to look in the mail for money, but sitting in a huge pile of junk mail next to the dog's water bowl was a treasure trove of money I had been ignoring for months. (If you're wondering why my mail is next to the dog dish, it's because she used to pay the bills for us. But I found out a couple of months ago the dog had no real head for finance and besides, she was secretly buying mail-order doggie treats using our checkbook.)

Anyway, in the pile of cast-off junk mail, I found our salvation.

The first two letters I picked up were from credit card companies offering me $75,000 to $100,000 in instant cash, with no bothersome security checks. All I had to do was swear I hadn't robbed a bank or defrauded a credit card company in the past five months.

Well, I figured one out of two wasn't bad, and it was just a small bank anyway. (Note: If anyone from the FBI is reading this, I was just kidding. Honest.) So, I put these two financial offers on the side and wrote down $175,000 in my checkbook, figuring I could have the banks overnight the money to me.

The next pile of junk mail yielded three offers to take out home equity loans on my house for up to 100 percent of its value, less the outstanding mortgages. That's another $50 or $60 I figured — maybe a full $200 if I refinanced with all three companies and cut the grass to make the place look presentable. I wrote $150 in the deposit column. (It's too late in the year to start cutting grass now.)

Hidden under our collie's sleeping rug was a bundle of offers from telephone companies. (I think from the looks of it, the dog may have been planning to open her own telemarketing firm. I guess it's a good thing I took her credit card away after the Milk-Bone incident.)

Found money

Looking through the literature, it was amazing how much money I could save just by signing up with each telephone carrier and buying a bunch of their add-on services like Caller ID and Call Forwarding. It seemed I could get the biggest savings by installing a direct phone line to my bank so the phone companies could just take money out of my checking anytime they wanted without having to bother me with things like bills and receipts.

I signed up for everything. I estimated I would save about $800 a month which I could use as income. So I put that down in my check-book, too.

In the same stack of mail, I also found a computer disk that would allow me to get America OnLine and the Internet for free. Popping the disk into the computer and signing on, I was immediately bombarded with 150 offers to make money from my home without doing practically anything.

In no time at all, I signed up for three financially-rewarding, part-time careers. With the first I'm going to make up to $200,000 a year licking stamps for companies that don't have postage machines. The second is going to bring me $100,000 a year selling herbal weight-loss secrets from King Tut's tomb. And the third generates about $20,000 a month and all I had to do was send a check for $35 to something called "Money Go Round."

Boy, I'm lucky I found this stuff. And here I thought the Internet was full of scam artists.

It's doggone fraud

That put me at $780,915 to the good so far. Not bad for a morning's work, I figured. But there was more.

Sitting next to the dog's flea powder were several applications for small business loans neatly typed out in my name with paw print smudges on the edges. (Bad dog!) Since they were already filled out, I signed up for three loans totaling $65,000 to get some cash flow go-ing for my fledgling businesses.

Along with the business loan applications, I found a stack of credit card checks worth about $38,000 made out to me. They were advances on credit card accounts someone had opened in my name. (I'm starting to see a pattern forming here.) Anyway, that's another $38,000 I didn't know I had.

I looked for more "found" money in the mail, but the rest of the stuff turned out to be just junk — the kids' report cards, overdue bills and a bunch of mail-order catalogs my wife had been missing for months. (I suspect the dog also had something to do with this, since several "Poodle" skirts and an ID bracelet with "Lassie" engraved on it were circled in one of the catalogs.)

Having gone through the whole pile of mail, I got the feeling something was still missing. Rummaging around in our collie's pile of old doggie toys, I discovered what I was looking for. It was my guaranteed $1 million check from the Publisher's Clearing House Sweepstakes. It was tied up in a brand new, diamond-studded dog collar along with a dozen Caribbean cruise brochures.

That was the last straw. I don't mind the dog trying to commit mail fraud against me, but taking my Publisher's Clearing House Sweepstakes was too much. That pooch is going spend a month in the dog house right after she gets back from Las Vegas.

> **"The only thing near a full-function universal remote control**
> **we have in the house is the garage door opener,**
> **which can shut off the TV, VCR and stereo**
> **all at the same time and open the**
> **garage door too."**

MY LIFE IS AN ELECTRONIC NIGHTMARE

We have a new entertainment center in our house with digital equalizers, surround sound, a VCR with numeric-code programming and a cable-ready stereo TV that allows on-screen digital display of controls.

We also have a remote-controlled multi-disc, state-of-the-art compact disc player and a Pentium 1.5 bigabyte Internet-ready, 3D graphic accelerated computer.

I'm not bragging. This is a plea for help.

Can someone out there show us how to use these things?

Six months ago, our lives were simple, almost idyllic. We had a 7-year-old TV that turned on manually and adjusted with a few simple knobs on the back of the set. We could change channels, adjust volume and play the VCR with one universal remote control that we bought at a garage sale.

The stereo, with its 45 RPM record changer and eight-track tape player, could bring forth our favorite tunes at a push of a button. And our computer, an old Apple that worked at a snail's pace and performed functions while you took a stroll around the block, allowed us to write letters and print them out.

The nightmare begins

Today, through an unfortunate series of equipment breakdowns, new purchases, and gifts from our loving children, our life has become an electronic nightmare.

The surround-sound speakers, when turned on, produce static from every corner of the room. The CD player is permanently stuck on Weird Al Yankovic singing "Polka Your Eyes Out." And the VCR rejects our taste in movies.

The other day, I tried to raise the volume on the TV set and somehow opened this 6-inch-high, on-screen programming box. Trying to shut it off so we could see the TV screen better, I accidentally opened the closed-caption box that prints what the actors are saying across the bottom of the screen.

Which was OK, because since we couldn't hear the sound, at least we could sit back on the couch and read the dialogue while we followed the action around the edges of the on-screen programming and closed-caption boxes.

It wasn't a perfect solution, but one I felt we could learn to live with. Except I couldn't leave well enough alone. While my wife, Madeline, pleaded with me to drop the remote control — "please for the sake of me and the children, don't do anything more," — I foolhardily tried to shut down the programming box, but all I managed to do was open up a few more boxes and change the closed captions from English to French.

So now we sit, huddled at the TV set, trying to watch "Rocky III" around the edges of all these on-screen boxes while Sylvester Stallone mouths: "Yo! Mon amie, bon jour."

Part of the problem is that every electronic device comes with its own remote control. Because we never threw out the old ones, we now have nine remote controls on our coffee table. One remote controls the static on the surround-sound speakers, a second remote shuts off Weird Al and a third allows us to add more boxes to the TV screen.

A universal remote

The only thing near a full-function universal remote we have in the house is the garage door opener, which can shut off the TV, VCR and stereo all at the same time and open the garage door, too.

If these problems were limited to the family room, I think I could live with it, but electronic computer-controlled logic has invaded every aspect of our lives.

My new computer can do 1,000 different processes in the blink of an eye, but it won't let me type a letter or print it out. We send e-mail to people by taking it to the post office and mailing it to them in a letter.

About the only computer program I can open is a game called 'Mime Hunter,' with which I can shoot mimes with a tomato gun.

In our kitchen, we have a self-cleaning oven that has never cleaned itself. We're afraid if we use it, a small puppy might somehow get trapped inside and we wouldn't be able to get it out until the 'incinerate' cycle was complete.

During the winter, we walk around the house in overcoats because our programmable thermostat, which controls the heat, turns it on during the day when no one is home and shuts it off at night when we walk in the door.

The microwave cools off our food. And our answering machine won't take messages. The only electrical appliance I can still run is the toaster, and I live in fear that someday it will break down and I'll have to buy a new one. If we don't get some help soon, you may find us one day frozen in our overcoats, huddled around the TV set while Weird Al sings "Polka Your Eyes Out."

"We talked about names for the new computer. My wife liked the newer names like Activa, Performa and Primavera, while I favored the old fashioned names like XT, Z-100 and PT-109."

BEGETTING A COMPUTER

Buying a computer is a lot like having a baby, my wife and I recently discovered. We came to this conclusion as we went through months of emotional decision making and delivery pains in buying our second computer.

Unlike our last computer, which just kind of happened, we actually planned this computer. It all started one night when my wife, Madeline, out of the clear blue, suggested it was time for another computer.

"It's been six years since our last one, and you don't want to wait too long between computers," she said.

"And you were so good with the last one," she said, snuggling in close. "I remember how you changed its floppy disks and would sit up with it all night when it got sick and began spitting out data."

"But a computer can be a big expense," I said. "I think we better make sure we can afford one first."

Never too old for a computer

Besides the expense of a new computer, there was another thing we had to take into consideration. My wife and I are a little beyond the prime computer buying years, and I was a bit concerned our age might work against us.

So, before we made our decision, we went out and consulted some experts.

"You've got nothing to fear," the computer dealers told us. "With the technology that exists today, you're never too old to have a new computer."

Still, I wasn't convinced. We were just reaching the point where our kids were going off to college and we could start enjoying our newfound freedom. I didn't know whether I wanted once again to be tied down by a new computer in the house.

They can be quite demanding of your time. You have to play computer games with them, and take them surfing on the Internet, then there's tee-ball and ballet classes. I just didn't know if I wanted to get back into that.

So we went out and collected all the information we could on computers, and then at home, behind closed doors, we did it. We went and bought a computer, mail-order.

Picking out names

Then we sat back and waited nine months for delivery. Actually, it was only a week, but it seemed much longer. While we waited, my wife and I did the usual things expectant parents do.

We talked about names for the new computer. She liked the newer names like Activa, Performa and Primavera, while I favored the old-fashioned names like XT, Z-100 and PT-109.

We also went out and took classes and bought all the books we could find on the care and feeding of computers. By the time we were done, we knew more about computers than we ever did about raising children.

One day, mid-way in the gestation period, I came home to find my wife wallpapering the computer room.

"I'm not bringing a new computer into our house with this old wall paper," she said firmly.

"And we're buying new computer furniture, too. No hand-me-downs from the last computer," she said, throwing away the folding chair and wobbly card table that had supported our old computer for so long.

Finally, the big day arrived and they delivered our computer. Except for writing the check, the delivery was practically painless.

Gently, we unwrapped our new bundle of joy and set it down tenderly in its room, which was decorated in new pink and blue AscII wall paper. While we counted the 101 keys on its keyboard, and checked its memory functions, it smiled up at us. We felt such joy. Our new baby was home — a strapping 40-pounder that is smart as a whip, can talk and is ready to do my taxes.

As we stood there looking with pride at our new addition, my wife put her head on my shoulder and mused: "Now that we have a new computer, maybe we should start thinking about getting a bigger house."

Chapter VII

THE YEAR IN REVIEW

The year seems to go by so fast it's important to stop once and a while and reflect on what has happened......Well, that's long enough, time to turn the page.

"As reports of Mad Cow disease put people off their feed in England again this year, a lesser-known epidemic of Disgruntled Chicken Disease hit this country in February, putting thousands of people in a fowl mood after dining on the infected birds."

LESSER-KNOWN EVENTS OF 1997

The end of the year news has been full of stories recounting the major events that filled 1997—as if we want to go through all that stuff again. Rather than rehash old news, this New Year's Day I'm touting the lesser-known historic events of 1997, some of which are actually true.

Starting with orbital news, while ongoing troubles with the Russian space station "Mir" filled the headlines almost daily this year, a lesser-known satellite, "Murph," from the small country of Legos went about its business almost trouble free. The only problem the Legos had was not being able to lift the seven ton satellite into orbit with hot air balloons.

So instead, they made an "Earth Station" out of Murph, which now sits in a cow pasture beside the launch site, rotating around the sun every 365 days. Both the "Murphanauts" and livestock are reportedly doing well.

As reports of Mad Cow disease put people off their feed in England again this year, a lesser-known epidemic of Disgruntled Chicken Disease hit this country in February, putting thousands of people in a fowl mood after dining on the infected birds.

Speaking of dining out, after Mike Tyson was banished from the human race for biting off part of the ear of defending boxing champ Evander Holyfield, lesser-known sports figure Elmo "the Fang" Leonard shocked title defender Clovis "Chomper" Wadson in the National "Biting" championship, when Leonard punched his opponent with a fist and knocked out a tooth.

Staying with sports for the moment, as big league football teams moved to computers to predict plays, Youngstown State University Penguins (no joke, that's their name) won a fourth national NCAA Division 1AA title with a play the YSU coaches drew in the dirt.

Who we gonna beat?

And chess Grand Master Garry Kasparov lost his battle with IBM super computer "Big Blue," but I finally won a game of Donkey Kong on my ColecoVision. The score now stands at Kukla "1" Donkey Kong "4,873."

"El Nino" has grabbed all the headlines this past year for disturbing weather trends, but a lesser-known force called "El Spartanos" managed to wreak havoc for Pennsylvanians during Thanksgiving, only to move on to Hawaii to ruin Christmas Day for some people in Michigan.

The Internal Revenue Service was exposed and chastised this year as a bully for harassing innocent taxpayers for fun and profit. Not as publicized was the reassignment of Internal Revenue under the Federal Alcohol, Firearms and Tobacco Enforcement Division, which will now allow the IRS to blow up your house for late filing of taxes.

On the genetic engineering front, Scottish scientists this year made world news with the announcement of a cloned sheep. Left in the dust, though, was the claim by an Albanian farmer to have cloned wheat. "Look at it," insisted the proud farmer. "It all looks alike, doesn't it." Except he said it in Albanian.

Former President George Bush made headlines in 1997 when he parachuted out of an airplane to celebrate Ground Hog's Day. Not so well known was former President Gerald Ford's leap from a moving golf cart to retrieve a lost head cover. Reported Ford after the historic jump, "If I'd have known it was that easy, I would have done it sooner."

It was the year of the smoking coffee grounds in the White House, in which foreign nationals allegedly traded big bundles of money for Sanka. Lesser known was the Pentagon scandal where America's military secrets were stolen by a Russian mole, who was paid in Monopoly money. The spy didn't realize the cold war had ended, or that Boardwalk and Park Place were already owned.

Industry unrest

United Parcel Service hourly employees tied up transit of millions of useless mail order purchases this year by going on strike. Not as widely recognized as the UPS strike was the slowdown at national burger outlets in the delivery of "fast food" orders. Most customers said they couldn't tell any difference since the orders still arrived cold and incorrect.

Big tobacco companies agreed to billion dollar settlements this year after one of their brethren broke ranks and announced "yes, smoking is not good for you." Lesser known was the milk industry settlement of a million-gallon class action suit brought by disgruntled customers who were unable to produce "milk mustaches" after drinking the product.

Democratic campaign fund raising videos destined for broadcast in Japan and Taiwan and showing the new Starbucks coffee shop at the Whitehouse—where coffee and a Danish are only $50,000—totally overshadowed the lesser publicized White House scandal where President Clinton traded the state of Rhode Island to the NFL for a future first round draft pick for the Washington Redskins.

On Wall Street, the Dow Jones ended the year like yo-yo. The losses, though, were nothing compared to the drop felt by investors who stockpiled "Tickle Me Elmo" dolls in hopes of cornering the market on last year's rare commodity.

This year saw literally thousands head for Washington D.C. almost weekly for the Million Man/Woman/Promisekeeper/UPS driver marches, but more admirable and less publicized were those who stayed home and went about their lives being good human beings without the aid of television interviews.

And finally, this was also the year the "Paparazzi" pursued Princess Di to her grave and Mother Teresa passed on to her reward. Two deaths which made everything else seem lesser for a while.

"Unwise as I was to the ways of the world, I didn't realize the guy had to pay for a corsage. I just assumed corsages came with the girl. What a dumb system, I thought."

VALENTINE'S DAY DANCE

Valentine's Day has always had a special place in my heart among holidays.

That's because I learned some very important lessons about life one Valentine's Day many years ago.

One was a lesson I'd never forget: Girlfriends cost money.

You have to remember this happened in a time before political correctness; a time before the Equal Rights Amendment; a time before I had a job and money.

I was in the sixth grade and just coming out of that awkward stage where boys think it's fun to show girls bugs, and just moving into that next stage where guys do other stupid things instead.

There was this girl Rosemary, who used to wear her beautiful brown hair in those ringlets that were popular in those days before styling moosh. I had admired her from afar since we were in the fourth grade. Well, it wasn't that far afar. We sat beside each other in class.

I can remember even now how daintily she ate her crustless peanut butter and jelly sandwiches at lunch and how amazed I was that anyone could be so neat. I actually had decided in the fourth grade to ask her out, but had waited a few years so as not to appear over-eager.

The big dance

Our school that year was throwing this big Valentine's Day dance in the gym. It was to be the social event of the season for all the sixth and seventh graders.

Somehow, I managed to talk to Rosemary without a bug in my hand and ask her to the dance. And with the faintest hint of blush on her cheeks and a demure smile on her face, she agreed.

I was the happiest boy in St. John's School that day. I literally floated home on air, carried by cherubs while Cupid tossed rose-petal hearts before me.

Sauntering into the house, I announced as casually as I could that I would be going to the school dance on Saturday with Rosemary.

"You're going to have to get her a corsage," said my father, not looking up from his evening paper. "Girls like corsages."

This was something I hadn't planned on. Unwise as I was to the ways of the world, I didn't realize the guy had to pay for a corsage. I just assumed corsages came with the girl. What a dumb system, I thought.

On the day of the dance, I pulled out my life savings of $5.78, which I had put away to buy a pocket knife. "Oh, well, this is for the love of your life," I thought, stuffing the money into my pocket and heading out for the florist shop.

Now I have to say on a scale of 1 to 100 of the most useful things in the world, flowers hadn't ever made my list. Entering the florist shop that day, I had no idea of what I was going to do. Luckily, the florist seemed to know something about flowers and recommended I buy a red-tinted chrysanthemum with my school's letter on it.

"She'll love it," he advised me. It's a good thing he was there to help, because left to my own instincts, I probably would have bought her a potted geranium, or a flowering shrub or something.

The corsage cost $2, which was a lot cheaper than a flowering shrub, and I felt pretty good as I headed home with my tissue paper wrapped, red-tinted chrysanthemum in its heart-covered florist box.

Back at home, with all of the naive delight of a schoolboy, I showed my mother the corsage and she said, "Did you remember to get some candy for her mother? They like that, you know."

It still amazes me that as wise as my parents were in the social graces of the day, it never occurred to them that I had no money to pay for these things.

Trudging down to the local corner store — with the remainder of my pocket knife fund — I bought not one but three boxes of candy. One for Rosemary, one for her mother and one for my mother. I wasn't taking any chances this time, unless the girl's father was owed some sort of Valentine tribute. If so, he was out of luck.

My dad drove me to Rosemary's home to pick her up. I have to say she was a dream in her organdy taffeta party dress, and with as much aplomb as I could muster, I distributed the gifts. I even pinned the corsage to the top shoulder of her dress without causing her any pain.

I'd like to say the evening was a huge romantic success. Actually, for most of the evening, the girls huddled on one side of the gym comparing chrysanthemums while the boys stood on the other side complaining about how much this dance had cost them. It was my guess that this one evening had thrown the pocket knife industry in our town into decline, if not outright collapse.

As the evening wound down to its final dance, I found myself at last alone with Rosemary, dancing to a slow song in a dimly lit corner of the gym. As the strains of the last dance came to an end, Rosemary looked up at me and said "Thank you" and gave me my first kiss.

And at that moment, I learned there were more important things in life than pocket knives.

"Although we can count on at least a thunderstorm every time we plan one of these picnics, that hasn't stopped us from optimistically predicting, "Maybe it will be nice this year."

PACK THE LIFE RAFTS, IT'S THE 4TH OF JULY

Well, it's time to get ready for the annual family 4th of July picnic.

I'm packing up the umbrellas, rain slickers, hip boots and the small rubber life raft we usually take to these gatherings. I'm not saying it always rains when we have a 4th of July picnic. Sometimes it hails and floods, too.

Remember the Great Flood in the Bible? That started on the day of one of my ancestor's July 4th shindigs.

While other families have Independence Day picnic pictures of freckle-faced kids eating hot dogs on a sunny afternoon, our photo album depicts our huddled masses in leaky picnic shelters, under blankets and plastic table cloths, while our cars float away in the background.

Although we can count on at least a thunderstorm every time we plan one of these picnics, that hasn't stopped us once from optimistically predicting, "Maybe it will be nice this year."

For us, it has become a challenge against nature to see how far we can get into the picnic before the deluge hits. Once we actually got the hamburgers off the grill and onto the buns before a typhoon came sweeping through the park and we had to turn the picnic tables into a makeshift shelter for the night.

Don't fool with Mother Nature

In the past, we've tried to fool Mother Nature by moving these picnics to various family members' homes across North America, but the storms always seem to find us.

I remember the 4th of July we had the big family picnic at our house here in Michigan.

We awoke that morning to a tornado passing through our back yard.

As tree branches crashed to the ground and rainwater flooded the streets and yards, my wife said, "It's a good thing we're having this tornado early, so it won't spoil the picnic."

She was right. We didn't get any rain that day, but the flash flooding through our back yard made it really difficult to grill and it was almost impossible to get a decent game of volleyball going among all the fallen trees.

One year, we decided to keep the location of our family picnic secret until last possible moment to throw off the weather. Everyone just got instructions to pack up the potato salad and cold cuts and start driving towards the North Carolina border, where we were to get further instructions.

At the border, we were handed a sealed envelope with a map to my brother-in-law's house in Sunset Beach, North Carolina. That's on the coast, just north of Myrtle Beach.

As we headed for the coast, the National Weather Service announced that Hurricane Bertha, with winds reaching 110 miles per hour, would be hitting land at my brother-in-law's house sometime later that afternoon.

"We've seen worse," I announced, stepping on the gas in hopes of getting there in time for a few innings of softball before the hurricane hit.

Run for your lives

I was really looking forward to this picnic because we had plans to finish the sack race we started in 1993. I was leading the race that year and was about 30 yards from the finish line when the mud slide occurred.

Anyway, when we were about halfway across the state, the governor of North Carolina announced that all coastal cities were being evacuated, and anyone having a family picnic there should also stay away.

The Weather Service also announced the possibility of a tidal wave hitting the coast.

"Oh goody," cried my youngest. "We've never had a tidal wave hit one of our picnics."

As we got closer to my brother-in-law's house, I turned on the radio for another weather update.

"The National Weather Service is advising all coastal residents to run for their lives," said the announcer. "And please feel free to panic if necessary."

As we approached the beach community where the picnic was to be held, we came across tens of thousands of people fleeing the oncoming hurricane. The one positive aspect of the evacuation was that all the cars were leaving town, so we didn't have much traffic as we pushed on towards our date with Hurricane Bertha.

It was just like being in one of those old monster movies where everyone in the world is fleeing the city as Godzilla attacks. Cars leaving town were bumper-to-bumper. People were running down the road, screaming from the oncoming terror. And there we were, driving along looking for a place to buy charcoal for the picnic.

At one point we got lost, so I stopped to ask directions.

"Pardon me sir," I said, hailing down a police officer. "Can you tell me where the hurricane is going to strike? We'd like to be there when it happens."

When we finally reached our destination, the wind was topping out at 96 miles per hour. We exchanged hugs and kisses with the relatives on the lawn as we tried to catch small children blowing by.

My brother-in-law had built a bunker for the picnic, and we all huddled inside watching the storm through eye slits in the reinforced concrete walls. We saw a couple trees and a small truck fly by and decided it wasn't going to be that bad of a storm at all.

"This is nothing compared to the storm that picked our cabin cruiser out of Lake Erie and dropped it in downtown Cleveland," said cousin Joey, remembering the 4th of July picnic of 1987.

I'm looking forward to this year's bash. We're holding it in northeast Ohio. So if you want to have a safe and happy 4th, just stay out of northeast Ohio if you know what's good for you.

"I had always thought roasting chestnuts on an open fire was just a whimsical expression, you know, like "Jack Frost nipping at your nose." I didn't know people actually cooked nuts on a fire. "

SURVIVING THE HOLIDAYS

Well the holiday season has come and gone and we've created another family Christmas memory that will last for many years to come.

It happened on Christmas day, when my wife innocently announced it might be nice to roast some marshmallows on the yule log.

At least that's the way I heard it, and several survivors agree that that would have been a much better idea than what transpired.

Instead, as we waited for Christmas dinner to finish cooking, my wife, Madeline, brought out a box of chestnuts and announced we were going to roast them on an open fire, just like in the "Christmas Song."

I had always thought roasting chestnuts on an open fire was just a whimsical expression, you know, like "Jack Frost nipping at your nose." I didn't know people actually cooked nuts on a fire.

"Why don't we just heat them in the microwave?" I asked, hoping to get out of building an actual chestnut-roasting fire. "Or maybe we could barbecue them on the gas grill," I suggested.

Since neither of those suggestions fit with the song lyrics, I dutifully set up a roaring fire in the fireplace while Mrs. Claus — as we sometimes call her at Christmas — prepared the chestnuts in the kitchen.

Watching chestnuts roast

Thinking I might be able to catch a cat nap while the chestnuts cooked, I headed for the family room.

"Where do you think you're going?" she asked.

"I'm going to watch a little TV with my eyes closed," I said.

"Wrong, you and the boys and I are going to watch these chestnuts roast on the open fire," she said, shaking a pan full of round, brown nuts in my direction. "It will be an experience we'll all remember. Now go get the boys," she said sweetly.

While I rounded up the kids, dragging them kicking and screaming from their video games to sit in the living room for a chestnut roasting party, my wife put the pan into the fire and explained the significance of the event.

"This is a tradition that goes back to merry ol' England when people would gather nuts and berries from the woods for their Christmas feast," she informed us.

"Wait a minute," cried our oldest son. "This isn't going to be like last year when you made traditional English Christmas pudding and we had to watch water boil for six hours."

Before she could answer, the first chestnut exploded, hitting me in the shoulder with shattered nut fragments.

"Are they supposed to do that?" I asked, scraping molten nut mush from my sweater.

"That was probably just a defective one," she assured me as two more went off, ricocheting pieces of nut meat and razor sharp chestnut shells off the ceiling and walls.

"Wow, cool," said our son Nathan, who was pinned to the wall by shell fragments.

Three more exploding chestnuts broke Christmas ornaments and shattered a lamp.

"Everybody, hit the floor!" I yelled, as a barrage of roasting chestnuts exploded from the fireplace, sending a fiery arch of burning squirrel food across the room.

My wife and I dove behind the sofa as more missiles went off. The three boys overturned the coffee table and threw a love seat on top for protection.

"Sing that song about the chestnuts again. I don't remember this part where everybody runs for their lives," I said, as we covered our head with pillows.

"Who gave you these things? The Unabomber?" asked our son Matt, a trained Ninja, as he crawled across the room to call 911.

One good thing I discovered about exploding chestnuts: they do it very quickly. It's like boom, boom, boom and it's over.

As we mopped up nut shrapnel from the walls and furniture, the bomb disposal expert from the state police determined that the chestnut shells had not been punctured prior to placement on an open fire as required by law.

"Thus undue pressure was allowed to build up within the nut during cooking, resulting in their exploding in your living room," he said.

"Better to stick to your pre-shelled nuts from now on, folks. They're much less combustible," called the disposal guy as he hopped into his van and headed out to another house where a partridge and two turtle doves had escaped from a pear tree, wedged themselves up the fireplace, and exploded.

" I decided what I really wanted for Father's Day was to have
life be like a VCR: that way I could go back and relive
some of the wonderful moments of my life
that I've shared with my family. "

I WANT LIFE TO BE LIKE A VCR

My sons recently asked me what I wanted as a present for Father's Day.

After running through my usual list of "peace on earth," a sports car and a speed boat — all of which they groaned at — I decided what I really wanted for Father's Day was to have life be like a VCR: that way I could go back and relive some of the wonderful moments of my life that I've shared with my family.

So the kids said "OK" and sprinkled some magic dust on my head, and sure enough my life rewound to a few days before my first son was born.

In the first tape, my wife Madeline and I are out on a picnic. We're sitting on a blanket under a tree. It's a beautiful day. Madeline is about 12 months pregnant and wearing a blue top with white shorts. The birds are singing. Clouds pass overhead, pushed along on their way by a soft breeze. We laugh and talk about the future as the day dwindles down to a perfect sunset.

That's the last quiet moment the two of us ever have on the tape.

In the next image of my life video, I'm in the waiting room of the hospital's maternity ward. Madeline is in delivery and I'm doing what fathers are supposed to do — waiting. I have everything I need for an extended stay — pop, candy, magazines, even books if the delivery is a long one. But the nurse walks in and says, "We're ready for you now. You can change in the doctors' dressing area and then come into delivery ."

"There's been a mistake," I protest. "I didn't sign on for any delivery. This was supposed to be a one-woman job. I'm just planning to wait out here and pace the floor manfully. That's my job."

She pushes me towards the dressing room, laughing.

"You'll do fine," she says.

"Look, I'm clumsy," I stammer. "I could drop something important."

Doctor! Doctor! Give me the news

While I'm in the dressing room trying to figure out how to get into the green operating cloths, our family doctor comes in and says "Hi" and starts getting undressed. He strips down to his blue Speedo underwear and slips into the loose fitting garments. I wonder briefly if Speedos are approved by the American Medical Association for child delivery and whether I want some guy in slinky underwear bringing our first child into the world.

But there's no time to debate this. The nurse pushes open the door and announces that the baby is coming.

Inside the delivery room, my wife is half sitting up on a the delivery table in one of those stylish hospital gowns with the open back. I kiss her and take her hand. She squeezes it gently. Then she squeezes it a little harder each time there's a contraction. For the next 20 minutes of my life's video all I can see is my left hand turning blue up to the elbow as she squeezes it to a pulp.

Then suddenly there's our baby. He looks just like my dad with his sleepy eyes and bald head. They wrap him in a towel and give him to Madeline. I tell her he's beautiful. We call him Jason, which means "stubborn little tyke, with a mind of his own."

The next scene is a year later. We now call Jason "Baby Houdini" because he can disappear from sight right before your eyes. Jason seems to have one mission in life: to run in a straight line until he reaches the horizon.

In one scene we're out shopping with Jason at a mall at Christmas time. Crowds are everywhere. The camera picks up mom and dad standing beside the empty stroller where Jason was sitting a second ago.

See his parents running through the mall frantically calling his name. See us find him sitting on the lap of a policeman.

See us thank the nice policeman. See us buy Jason a nice child harness for Christmas to keep him strapped in his seat.

Look out here they come

It's spring again. Time for a new baby and here comes Nathan. His name means "Gift of God." That's why his mother thinks we picked the name. Actually, I named him after a bookmaker I owed money to, who was so touched he forgave the debt. But don't tell his mom that.

As with most second children, there are not as many early pictures of Nathan on my life cassette as there are of Jason. There's shots of me wrestling with the boys on the dining room floor — two babies beating up their dad. Then there's a shot of mom trying to comb Nathan's duck-down fine hair and it fluffing back out again. And here's a shot of Nathan teaching his brother how to climb things so the two of them can get at all the good stuff their parents have hidden in high places.

Wait, here comes your brother Matthew, a Christmas baby. Lucky for him, I swore off gambling. The new bookie in town is named Bubba. We take Matthew home and put him under the Christmas tree like a present. Here's me saving Matthew when the tree starts falling over.

The tape picks up a year later. It is Matt's first birthday and I bring home a dog as a present to round out the family. We call the dog "Browny," which means "most untrainable dog in the world." When he's not chewing up shoes and toys, he's trying to run away from our happy home.

There's a shot of me waking up one morning and looking out the front window to see Browny running down the street, chased by Jason, who is being chased by Nathan. And all three are being chased by mom.

A big Michigan welcome

We've moved to Michigan in the next scene. The Midwest welcomes us with a tornado. It is early morning and my wife wakes me, shouting, "The kids are screaming they are being sucked out the window." We run to their rescue. Only later in the shelter of the basement do I find out what she was really saying was "the kids' screens are being sucked out the window" and we laugh.

I have a whole cassette in my mind of nothing but birthday parties we threw for the boys on our screened-in porch. Years being counted away by the number of candles on their birthday cakes. Even Matt gets warm weather, mid-year birthday parties there to make up for the presents he loses each year being a Christmas baby.

I've also got a cassette of Halloween memories. Shots of the boys as soldiers, football players and gun-slingers. Then there's the year they dressed up to look like their favorite television cartoon heroes "HeMan" and "Battlecat" and someone who looks like a Cabbage Patch Doll, although I don't know how that character got in there.

As the video memories spin by, they seem to pick up speed, jumping from one subject to another: Jason as Santa Claus in his school play; Nathan winning a 4-H prize; Matt playing GI Joe; Jason going off to school; Nathan doing skate-board tricks; Matt getting his first deer. In between, there's shots of mom and dad. In some we're beaming, in others we have these worried looks on our faces. Those shots alternate back and forth.

The girls start appearing

Then girls begin appearing in my life's video. We didn't have any girls, but they seem to be in my movies anyway. At first there's little girls with braces and pigtails. Then, like the seasons, they begin to change — from schoolgirls in jumpers, to cheerleaders with pompons to young ladies in formal dresses — all standing with our boys.

There's proms, and homecomings, baseball games and football games. We win, we lose, we win, we lose again. Track meets whiz by at the speed of an 80 meter dash. We applaud the good plays, we cheer when they score, we clap and our hearts burst with pride at the athletic awards banquets.

But there seems to be something wrong. The video-tape machine has gone into high gear. Suddenly there's a whirl of images one after another: A graduation, caps and gowns, a party, college packing, another graduation, another party.

"Wait," I shout, "I didn't see who that was." I try to slow the machine down but still it runs faster. The seasons rush across the screen in a blur of color. It's Christmas, it's Easter, it's summer, fall, winter and spring again, over and over. I search frantically for the pause button to slow this darn thing down, but there is no stopping it.

I guess when I think about it, I got my Father's Day wish. Life is like a VCR. But it's always stuck in fast forward.

Chapter VIII

THE OPEN ROAD IS CLOSED

Summer is my favorite time of year. Vacations, summer camp, the county fair, bad drivers, construction delays. On second thought, it's not summer I like so much but the memory of what summer used to be.

*"I wouldn't mind it so much if they actually did road construction,
but most of the traffic tie-ups I come across on highways seem
to be caused by barrels somebody has put out on the road,
in anticipation of construction occurring sometime
in the next century."*

THE OPEN ROAD IS CLOSED

There's nothing I like to do more in the summer then pile the family into the car and head out on the open road for vacation. We have been going on driving trips every summer since the kids were young. But, it seems these days that wherever we travel there is road construction going on.

I just got our trip maps from the automobile club for a July vacation the other day and every major highway I need to travel on to reach my destination has construction. Even the detours they recommend have construction. In fact, it was so bad the travel club attached a note saying "we think you should stay home this summer."

There's nothing worse than taking to the open road, only to find it closed. I wouldn't mind it so much if they actually did road construction, but most of the traffic tie-ups I come across on highways seem to be caused by barrels somebody has put out on the road, in anticipation of construction occurring sometime in the next century.

Nothing irks me more than to be crawling along at a brisk five-to-six miles per hour in a traffic tie up, while acres of perfectly good pavement I could be driving, sit unused behind traffic barrels. Sometimes I get the feeling that they put these barrels out there to fool us into thinking the road is under construction when it really isn't.

Roll out the barrels

I can just picture the head of the state highway construction projects talking to his summer crew. "Well, there's not much state money this summer for road construction, but the barrel fund is pretty flush," he says.

"So here's the plan," he whispers confidentially. "We'll put out 140 miles of barrels along the state roads and then take the summer off and go fishing." Obviously, they have to leave on a skeleton crew with equipment to make it look real, so they take volunteers to stay and work from the non-fishermen and those who want to get sun tans.

Then they rotate these crews to different locations across the state so it looks like there's a lot of construction activity occurring. I believe there may actually only be one work crew out for the whole Eastern seaboard and Midwest. They just move from state-to-state pretending to do road work.

Really, think about it. Don't all those road construction crews look exactly the same? For one thing, there is always a bulldozer pushing dirt around and behind it are eight men leaning on shovels. What do they need the shovels for? Will they take over if the bulldozer breaks down?

I can just see the shovel crew foreman going "All right guys, the dozer's out of commission so it's up to us to move that mountain up yonder."

Another common sight on road construction projects is the person who turns the signs. One side of the sign reads "Stop" and the other side reads "Go." This is so you know whether to stop or go.

This is a very tough job, usually handled by a big, burly guy that looks like he might be able to bench press small cars. Instead they've got him turning this little sign back and forth. I'll bet this guy goes home at night and complains, "What a day! I must have turned that sign 80 times. Boy, are my hands chaffed."

Tough jobs in construction

Another tough job on road construction projects is the guy who is required to stand in the middle of the work site with his foot on a pile of rocks while staring off into the distance. For some reason this appears to be a guys' job. Women just must not be strong enough to hold up a pile of rocks with their foot, I guess.

Women, though, often serve other functions on construction sites, like standing beside the road in yellow safety vests and hard hats with their hands on their hips, staring off into the distance. I think these jobs are apprentice positions to the job of "road pointer."

You've seen road pointers on construction projects. There are usually three of them, all wearing hardhats and holding a map. They stand out in the middle of a project and point off in three different directions. I see them all over the country wherever there is a road project. And it's always the same three people. I've become certain these aren't real people at all, just cardboard cutouts that they set out at various points along the construction route.

From what I can tell, the entry level job on all the construction sites is the guy who has to lean up against the pickup truck all day. There's always at least half a dozen of these jobs on every road construction job in America.

I'm not an expert on road construction, but I can't imagine this job requires much skill. In fact, I think workers sometimes send their relatives to fill in for them when they don't feel like working.

"Hey boss, Mike's sick today, so he sent me to fill in for him," says the construction recruit. "So what pickup truck do I have to lean against?"

Having recently spent a lot of time on the road in Ohio, I'm certain that every new driver in that state gets a card with their license that reads: "You are now an Ohio driver, please drive as goofy as you want." I know it did when I got my Ohio license. ❧

CAUTION: OHIO DRIVER ON BOARD

I was driving through heavy traffic the other day when the car in front of me cut over to the shoulder of the road and began passing cars while driving in the grassy median. The car then made a right turn across four lanes of traffic and parked at a bus stop.

When I caught up with the car I rolled down my window and shouted, "You can't drive like that, Mom, it's illegal."

She waved me off, laughing, "Sure I can, I've got an Ohio driver's license."

Having recently spent a lot of time on the road in Ohio, I'm certain that every new driver in that state gets a card with their license that reads: "You are now an Ohio driver, please drive as goofy as you want."

I know it did when I got my Ohio license.

I guess I've spent too much time out of the state, though, because now when I go back to Ohio, it looks like everyone is driving as if they're on one of those bumper car rides at an amusement park.

I've seen drivers in Ohio make left turns from the right lane, stop in the middle of the road to read maps, and drive across the median of a four-lane highway to get to a fruit stand.

I've even seen a car with Ohio plates go the wrong way through a McDonald's Drive Thru. I said, "What are they doing, dropping off hamburgers?"

At least my mother has an excuse for her bad driving. She's legally blind. But what about the rest of the people there?

Ohio drivers seem to think they own the passing lane on divided highways. They get in that left lane and just cruise along as slow as they please, making everyone pass them on the right. They should put signs up on the side of the road reading, "Left lane for Ohio drivers only. All others suffer."

Another strange driving quirk Ohio drivers have is an inability to pass trucks. In Michigan, we come up to a truck and we pass it. No messing around. In Ohio I've seen cars doing 80 miles an hour come up to a truck and put on their brakes.

They slow down to the exact speed of the truck and then creep forward at about a half-mile per hour faster than the truck is going. Then they get to the front of the truck and have to look both ways before pulling ahead. Well, considering they're driving in Ohio, that makes sense. Somebody might be driving through the median, crossing the highway headed for a fruit stand.

Ohio drivers also don't seem to understand the purpose of turn signals. They either don't use them when making turns or they leave their turn signal on all the time. You can see them driving down the highway for miles with their turn signals on like they're going to make a right-hand turn into a cornfield.

Old habits, new license
As for myself, I seem to have lost all my bad driving habits since moving to Michigan. The truth is they took them away. I had to retake the written driver's test when I moved here and that wasn't easy. I had all these bad habits that didn't match the answers on the driving test, so I had to make up my own answers.

Some of the questions went like this.

Q. When you come to a traffic light that has turned yellow you should?
A. Turn on your radio real loud, flash your lights and drive erratically so people know you're going through the light.

Q. If four cars come to a four-way stop at the same time, who has the right of way?
A. I do.

Q. A "Yield" sign means?
A. Other drivers should get out of my way.

Q. Children in the back seat of a car should be?
A. Quiet.

Q. The left lane of a divided highway is for?
A. Ohio drivers.

Q. Turn signals should be used when?
A. Passing your drivers test.

Q. What should you do at a railway crossing?
A. Always beat the train.

I thought that last one was very clever and practical. When I turned in my test results the lady behind the desk checked them and said, "You must be from Ohio."

When I told her I was, she made me turn in the card that allowed me to drive as goofy as I wanted and stamped it "Revoked" before she issued my Michigan license.

Michigan drivers have faults

I don't want to leave the impression that Michigan drivers are perfect. They also have a few quirky habits. Michigan drivers seem to like to see how close they can drive up behind your car at high speeds without actually touching your bumper. I swear that you could be driving in a cornfield at 3 a.m. at 60 mph and a car will pull up behind you and sit on your bumper and it will be a Michigan driver.

That happened to me once a long time ago before I came to Michigan.

I'm driving through a cornfield at 3 a.m. and this Michigan driver comes up right behind me. So I stop my car in this cornfield and go over to talk to the other driver.

"Why were you following me so close?" I asked.

"Because I didn't want to lose you in all this corn," he said.

"What are you doing driving in a cornfield at 3 a.m. anyway?" I asked.

"I'm lost and I thought you knew where you were going," he said.

Realizing how stupid that made him sound, he threw the question back at me.

"And what are you doing driving in a cornfield at 3 a.m.?" he asked sarcastically.

"Me?" I answered. "Why, I have an Ohio driver's license, I can drive as goofy as I want."

*"The moment my folks drove away from Camp Ivy,
the sun disappeared, a green slime spread over
the lake and the alligators began fighting
with bears in the underbrush."*

SUMMER AT CAMP POISON IVY

July always reminds me of summer camp. Probably because July and summer both fall at the same time I used to go to camp.

My first summer camp experience came when I was 10 and my parents packed me off to Camp Poison Ivy for a harrowing six days in the underbrush.

Camp Ivy, its official name, was used during World War II as a prisoner of war camp until it was closed for humanitarian reasons.

On the morning we arrived at Camp Ivy, the day was sunny, the lake glistened like a blue jewel and the whole place spoke of summer fun in the wilds.

"See. I told you this was a nice place and you had nothing to worry about," said my father, reassuring my mother's separation anxieties.

"The boy will have fun here," he declared.

The moment my folks drove away from Camp Ivy, the sun disappeared, a green slime spread over the lake and the alligators began fighting with bears in the underbrush.

All of us campers were herded into the main dining area for orientation where we received a short speech from the camp commander, a former military man named Col. Klink.

Have fun, or else!

"You will have fun here," he shouted. "Anyone who doesn't have fun, will get a day in the box. We'll also teach you water skills like canoeing and swimming. Anyone who doesn't learn a skill, gets a day in the box."

He went on like this for half an hour, never quite explaining what "the box" was, but leaving us the impression it was worse than our cabins, which were covered with moss and smelled like old sweat socks. After his speech, we were assigned to our cabin groups and given dinner. The main course was something that looked like mashed potatoes covered with green slime. It was called Camp Ivy Surprise. The surprise was that no one came down with food poisoning.

"I'm breaking out of the place," confided one of my cabinmates, as he stuffed table spoons into his pocket and checked a bus schedule he had hidden in his underpants.

After dinner we were supposed to roast marshmallows and sing songs around the campfire, but it was raining, so instead we watched slides of other kids sitting around the campfire singing songs and roasting marshmallows.

The cabin counselors at the camp all had names like "Biff" and "Todd" and "Bobby." Our counselor, though, was named "Snake." He said he was on a work-release program from the local penitentiary, and suggested we shouldn't make him mad or it might look bad on his probation record.

Snake got his nickname because he kept a bunch of live snakes in his room.

"Sometimes I leave them out here on the floor at night to feed," Snake confided. "I wouldn't want to be caught out of bed during the night if I were you."

Nobody left their bunks that night, not even to go to the bathroom. I was so glad I had taken an upper bunk.

Acid rain clears up the lake

The next morning the sun came out again. The slime was off the lake, killed by the acid rain from the nuclear power plant up the road. We had green oatmeal for breakfast and it was the first time I ever put ketchup on cereal.

Camp Ivy offered a rotating choice of activities for the campers that included archery, canoeing, leather crafts, hiking, and first-aid skills. My group started with the crafts class. All of us made knee-high leather moccasins the first day to ward off snake bite.

In the afternoon we got to go canoeing. They put all of us who had never been canoeing in a small, roped-off area of the lake. There were about 40 of us in 20 canoes in this tiny area and we just kept bumping into each other until we all overturned. Then they gave us all "expert" medals and told us to never go canoeing again.

I didn't eat much dinner that night. It looked like a combination of Camp Ivy Surprise with oatmeal over it. Again, no one got sick from the meal.

Trails are for wimps

The next morning Snake announced he was taking us on a nature hike, which was just as well since archery was canceled due to the many casualties from the day before, and the lake was covered with green slime again.

We were all assigned Quinine tablets and machetes for our trek through the woods. That's because Snake didn't believe in following trails.

"Trails are for sissies," he said, hacking his way into the underbrush.

Snake promised we would see wonders beyond belief on our hike. And we did. We saw an auto graveyard at the bottom of a cliff where people drove off their old DeSoto's and Plymouths, which was pretty cool.

We also saw swarms of mosquito so thick we had to cover ourselves with mud to keep from being eaten alive. That was really cool.

Snake also showed us some wilderness skills, like how to build a campfire with a Zippo lighter, dig tiger pits, build perimeter defenses and set land mines. We loved it.

Back at camp that night we found the cabin next to us had filled our beds with shaving cream. They even put shaving cream on the snakes. We wanted to retaliate immediately but Snake kept us back saying we'd get our revenge in good time.

I don't remember much about Wednesday at camp. They served us hamburgers and French fries for lunch and we all got sick and lapsed into a coma.

The next day was a drag too. One of the campers got lost in the woods and we spent the day looking for him. The kid really wasn't lost. He had simply tried to make a break for home. We found him in one of Snake's tiger pits covered with mosquitoes.

The big surprise

Friday was supposed to be the big day at Camp Ivy. That's when we took all of the skills we had learned at the camp and used them in competition among the different cabins. Since my group hadn't really learned anything at camp except how to put ketchup on everything we ate, we didn't do real well in the competition.

"That's okay," Snake assured us. "The big prize of the day is for trailblazing and you guys are experts at that."

Trailblazing consisted of following a combination of written clues and Indian signs through the woods that would lead us to the camp treasure. Each of the cabins got a different map that supposedly all led to the treasure.

As we clambered up the hill beside Camp Ivy looking for clues, Snake kept telling us, "Don't worry, it's in the bag."

To our surprise we reached the treasure chest first. It was an ice cooler filled with soda and candy bars hidden in a small cave at the top of the hill. Snake made us drag it out to a clearing overlooking the camp.

As we devoured our candy bars and sipped our Cokes, we saw down below, the creeps from the neighboring cabin that had shaving creamed our beds running toward the flagpole at the center of camp. A sack was tied at the top of the pole.

"We won, we won," they shouted, as the sack came down the pole.

We watched these guys gather around the sack to see what was inside. Suddenly they all began screaming and running for the lake as the distinct aroma of skunk spread through the camp.

"Revenge is so sweet," said Snake, biting into one of the candy bars as we all slapped him on the back laughing.

I went back to Camp Ivy the next summer, but it wasn't the same. Snake wasn't there anymore. He'd gotten paroled.

"My family had dragged me to the county fair to get a better appreciation of all the hard work done by our nation's farmers and see the Demolition Derby. What the connection is between growing fruits and vegetables and smashing up old cars has always escaped me."

MY FIRST LOVE SHOWED HER CALVES AT THE COUNTY FAIR

I don't know if it happens to you, but every once in awhile a certain smell or aroma will trigger a long-forgotten memory and take me back instantaneously to a certain place and time in my youth.

That happened to me recently when I went to our local County Fair. I was walking carefully through the livestock barn when the aroma of all those cows and horses hanging out together brought back memories of my first teenage love.

I don't mean to say she smelled like a barn. Well, actually she did, but in a pleasant way. You know, a sweet mix of new mown hay, honeysuckle and topsoil enricher.

She was a farm girl, a 4-H club member who had come to show off her calves at our annual fair. And they were beautiful, as were the two baby cows she had brought with her.

I'll never forget her name

I'll never forget her name, it was Abigail Something-or-Other and she had the prettiest strawberry blond hair, a clean-scrubbed face dotted with freckles, and a set of teeth so perfect and white that they sparkled when she smiled.

My family had dragged me to the fair to get a better appreciation of all the hard work done by our nation's farmers and see the Demolition Derby. What the connection is between growing fruits and vegetables and smashing up old cars has always escaped me, but it seems to be a tradition at every county fair I've ever attended.

We did all the big fair things that day. We walked through the wheat and grain exhibit marveling at how one bunch of wheat looks exactly like the next bunch of wheat. "How do they do that?" my father asked.

We saw the crafts show filled with more potholders than I've ever seen in my life, or ever care to see again. We went through the farm implement display, studying each and every John Deere tractor like we were going to buy one for our back yard.

After touring the canning and preserves display, where farm women competed with each other to see who could stuff the strangest things into a Mason jar — one blue ribbon was given for a batch of pickled eggs with Happy Faces etched on them — we finally arrived at the livestock pavilion.

I almost didn't go in there. One whiff of the place told me there were other places I'd rather be, but my mom and dad insisted that going through and seeing all the animals would be an "educational experience" for me, which usually meant I wasn't going to like it at all.

But about halfway through the display of animal hindquarters, I caught sight of Abigail. She was busy brushing down the fur on her cows, making them presentable for the next day's livestock judging.

She looked up at me and I smiled, and she smiled back. And I was in love. I could have stood in that livestock pavilion all day watching her groom her cows. Suddenly it was the most wonderful place in the world.

I want to become a farmer

I surprised my folks the next day when I said I wanted to go back to the fair again. "We were just there yesterday," Mom said with pure mom logic.

"I know, but I want to go back. I think I want ... I want to become a farmer," I said, offering up the most reasonable sounding explanation I could think of without telling the truth.

"I want to grow animals and herd wheat," I said, warming up to the idea. "In fact, I'm thinking of joining the 5-H Club at school next year."

My father wasn't buying any of it though. "Sounds to me like he's gotten interested in some young filly at the fair," explained my dad.

"Oh dear," said my mother, concern showing on her face. "You know we can't keep a horse here. The neighborhood's not zoned for farm animals."

I want to be a sick puppy

I wound up back at the fair that afternoon, and found my way back to Abigail and her cows. She was brushing their teeth or something when I stepped into the pen to introduce myself.

As I walked over to her, one of the cows stepped on my foot.

"Owwww," I said by way of introduction.

119

"Oh dear," she said, the sound of genuine concern in her voice. "I hope you haven't broken anything," she said rushing over to check on her cow's hind leg while I hopped around the pen holding my crushed foot.

When she was done tending to her cow, she made me sit down on some straw in the corner of the pen and take my shoe and sock off. Examining my foot, she declared it bruised but not broken. "Good, we won't have to shoot you," she joked. At least I think she was joking.

We spent the afternoon discussing life and animal husbandry. She said she wanted to be a veterinarian when she grew up and I told her I wanted to be a sick puppy.

I came back every day of the fair that week to be with Abigail. We walked the midway and shared French fries and ate giant red candy apples that stuck to the roof of our mouths and made us talk funny.

We rode the roller coaster and the Ferris wheel, and laughed at ourselves in the fun house mirrors.

During the week I met her parents and most of her family, including an aunt who had won a blue ribbon at the fair for her jar of pickled eggs with the happy faces etched on them.

The boyfriend bench-pressed dairy cows

I also met her ex-boyfriend Olaf, who bench-pressed dairy cows for exercise. He was upset with me because I was showing interest in Abigail. I assured him I was only interested in her calves but he said that was "a lot of bull' and tried to knock my head off with a single punch. But I was too quick for him and took a dive to the dirt before he could do me any permanent damage. He thought that was the funniest thing he had ever seen and left me alone after that, especially when Abigail threatened to take the sheep shears to him or something if he didn't behave.

What a girl! She was beautiful, smart, able to fend off bullies and raise beef for the freezer. Who could ask for anything more?

On the last night of the fair Abigail and I went alone to watch the fireworks. As the incendiary devices burst in the air above our heads, we kissed and promised our undying love for each other.

Well, not exactly. What we promised to do was stay in touch with each other. Maybe get together in the fall. But like so many summer romances, we wrote a few times and then went our separate ways.

It's too bad it worked out that way. I was really starting to get interested in animal husbandry.

*"I want summer back. Not the past 60 days of partly cloudy,
inclement weather that passed for summer. I want real
summers where sweet corn is knee high by the
4th of July and owning a convertible
is practically a necessity."*

THE LOST ART OF SUMMER

I want summer back. No, I'm not talking about the past 60 days of partly cloudy, inclement weather that passed for summer.

I want the real summers back.

I want the summers that made the tulips bloom on time. Summers when you didn't have to wear an overcoat to watch the Memorial Day parade.

I want the old fashioned kind of summers that started to heat up the days in May and by the first of June had us all hanging out of the schoolhouse windows waiting for freedom.

I want a summer where the sweet corn is knee high by the 4th of July.

I want the summers where it started getting hot before the sun came up, and just got warmer all day until the cicadas sang their last songs at dark.

I want the summers where you can see the heat rise from the pavement and know you could fry an egg there if you tried.

I want the kind of summer where people greeted one another at the start of each new day with the reminder "it's going to be another hot one."

I want those summers where you walked only the shadiest streets to get home, just to stay cool.

I want those hot summer days where ice cream cones would melt down your arm in rivulets of vanilla if you didn't eat them fast enough.

I want those summers where popsicles came from the freezer still covered with frost and stuck to your lips for an instant before cooling you from the inside out.

I want summers where when the rains came, it just got hotter.

I want the summers where lawns burned out so little kids didn't have to cut them anymore.

I want the summers that are so hot, hummingbirds would stop for a rest.

I want the kind of summer that makes owning a convertible practically a necessity.

I want the summers where you'd go to the movies just to cool off, and it didn't make any difference what was playing.

Summers of adventure

I want back summers where the days unfold like pages in an adventure book.

I want the summers where crawdaddies would hide in cool stream crevices, under rocks for little kids to find them.

I want the summers where screen doors slam, and little girls play hopscotch on the sidewalk.

I want the summers where "the livin' is easy, and the catfish are jumpin' all around."

I want the summers where you greeted neighbors and friends from front porch swings, toasting them with glasses of ice-cold lemonade.

I want the summers where you could sit back in the shade of a tall old maple and think about nothing.

I want the summers where there's nothing to do, but complain "there's nothing to do."

I want the summers where baseball games lasted all day, every day, and no one won, and no one cared.

I want the summers with family picnics and ice chests filled with food and Nehi pop.

I want the summers where mom's fresh-baked fruit pies never got a chance to cool.

I want the summers where the ice-cool watermelon juice ran down your chin as you tried to see how far you could spit the seeds.

I want the summers where you sat outside at night on vinyl kitchen chairs and listened to the Cubs lose another one.

I want the summers where you escaped the heat by running away to a lake-side cottage and then sweltered there in primitive happiness, under the cooling breeze of rattling window fan that had seen better days.

I want the summers where kids could sleep in backyard tents, safe under a blanket of stars.

I want the summer nights where it got so hot you moved your bed onto the screened-in porch and crickets lulled you to sleep.

I want summer nights back where you could lay listening to the mournful cry of far-off steam engines going to places you've never been.

I want summer nights where you'd prop up your transistor radio on the porch steps and listen to Chicago disc jockeys paint the evening with new rock and roll from the Coasters, Chuck Berry and the Drifters.

I want summers with drive-in movies.

I want summers back with the hint of romance, and long talks about the future.

I want back summers that last forever.

I want summer back.